Modern Commemorative Coins

Invest Today
Profit Tomorrow

FEATURING U.S. COINS
FROM 1982 TO DATE

Eric Jordan
Debbie Bradley, Contributing Editor

Published by

krause publications
A division of F+W Media, Inc.

700 East State Street • Iola, WI 54990-0001
715-445-2214 • 888-457-2873
www.shopnumismaster.com

To order books or other products call toll-free 1-800-258-0929
or visit www.shopnumismaster.com

Library of Congress Control Number: 2009937523
ISBN-13: 978-1-4402-1289-5
ISBN-10: 1-4402-1289-9

Cover design by Paul Birling
Interior design by Jana Tappa
Edited by Debbie Bradley

Printed in China

contents

Modern Commemorative Coins

Modern U.S. Coinage: Index of Topics

Disclaimer: Every reasonable effort has been made to provide accurate information in this text, but the reader must decide for his-or-her self how to best spend their collecting dollars. Favorable review of a coin does not guarantee its performance or return on investment. Coin prices can and do move in both directions sometimes resulting in profits or loss of capital.

f o r e w o r d

Fellow collectors,

I am a fourth generation collector who holds and perpetuates a set of coins from 1793 through 1964 that has very few gaps, so I understand what "legacy" means in every sense of the word. I have been an astute student of coins for more than 50 years and have had the benefit of three prior generations to get me to where I am today in my understanding of this thing we call a hobby.

With that said, I want to try to give you a realistic view of what is going on in the "legacy" and "modern" coin arenas. The legacy coins have been slowing down in popularity since about 1995. I could argue that point, but that is about the time that the real modern mania started and it has been accelerating ever since. *If you consider the fact that most legacy collections are almost impossible to even complete, much less complete in high grade, and then consider that moderns are attractive, rare and are at this point still completable (even though the window is getting narrow), it's obvious why we all should be paying attention to this area of the market.*

Take a 1907 $20 high relief Saint-Gaudens with a surviving mint state population of about 5,000 coins that has taken a hundred years to mature into the $10,000-$11,000 price range and compare it to mint state platinum eagles with their sub 3,000 mintages. As an owner of several varieties of the high relief Saint-Gaudens, I know that from an appreciation standpoint, the saint is pretty flat. As someone who just purchased several sets of the mint state platinum Eagles, they have just lifted off and you haven't seen anything yet. I will challenge you to look at any modern silver, gold, or platinum coin going and you will see what I mean by the "reality of things to come."

The Baby Boomers, or those people born prior to about 1955, have been the holders of most of America's wealth for a lot of years. I have seen them give rise to booms and busts in almost everything from the 1960s muscle cars to the current boom in nursing homes. These people have motivated inventions, driven markets of every description, and in general financed this country.

With that said, I have to bring into perspective that these people (like myself) are getting old and starting to die off. As this attrition deepens, there will be a shift in amounts of money and interest in what coins will be sought after and hoarded. *What you will see in the future is that the new breed of collector will come into the market, not with the perspective of "old" coins, but with the coins that he/she can relate to. This ultimately will be the moderns of today.*

I am not preaching the doom of legacy coins, I am just stating that life has a certain evolution that is inevitable. Collectors who fail to recognize these foreseeable changes will most assuredly find themselves facing unnecessary losses.

We are on the tail end of the "legacies" and the front end of the "moderns," *so if you have a little money, a few years in front you and do a little homework, the upside potential in well-selected moderns is very impressive.* This text is a good start on what you need to know to take advantage of the opportunities that modern U.S. coinage is offering us all today.

Sincerely,

Hank Swain

(Hank Swain is a fourth generation collector of U.S. coins.)

Wendy Jo and Eric Jordan

from the author

I started collecting coins in middle school during the early 1980s and had the privilege of working for Palmetto Galleries in Columbia, S.C., as a coin grader starting in late high school. My undergraduate studies were completed at North Carolina State's School of Engineering at Raleigh and it was at this point that I realized what I really enjoyed is the study of markets, their history and economics. These realizations led me to finish my graduate work at the University of South Carolina at Columbia's School of Business.

My formative collecting years were dominated by my interest in proof-like Morgan dollars, full bell line Franklin halves and to a certain extent classic commemoratives. Starting in the late 1990s, I realized that I was not going to be able to complete the proof-like Morgan set, which was my first love. Even if I did, the set's value indexed to inflation had leveled out or worse. This was a serious problem given that a significant percentage of my savings was in my coin collection.

Curiosity about all things related to U.S. numismatics and precious metals brought to my attention the radical drop in high-end modern coin mintages and the obvious low risk opportunity they presented. I had not started on my intense study of rare coin market history and modeling yet, but it was obvious that these new design-based coins had good genetics and were cheap. "You will never get hurt if you buy the good stuff cheap," my old mentor used to tell me.

It was about this time that I began comparing notes with a highly competent and forward thinking fourth generation collector named

Hank Swain. It is through hours of discussion with him and other experienced collectors and dealers, such as Dan Knauth, that the primary concepts seen in this text began to take form. Michael White, Judy Dixon and other U.S. Mint Office of Public Affairs personnel have been helpful with data acquisition.

I kept several things in mind during the seemingly endless hours it took to complete this research. They are:

"He who is taught only by himself had a fool as his master."
– Ben Johnson

"What we think isn't as important as why we think it."
– Unknown

"No one can play at this level without the help of others."
– Coach Bryant

So I would like to take this opportunity to thank my wife Wendy Jo for putting up with the endless hours of study needed to complete this text, my parents Buck and Sandy Jordan, my grandparents Bob and Nora Rice and my brother Brian's family for their love and support. Most of all I would like to thank Jesus for his unfailing love and mercy.

Sincerely,

Eric Jordan

P.S. This text is written to those who want to have a better shot at recognizing and buying Secretariats for the stable long before they have won the Triple Crown and then holding them to produce ultra long cycle taxable events that are likely to benefit succeeding generations.

introduction

Yesterday's Modern Issues
are Today's Great Classic Coinage

If you had the opportunity to collect coins on a limited budget from 1906 to 1936 would you have seen the astounding opportunity that moderns presented at that time? Would you have actively sought out the deep mintage keys in the midst of a series with rapidly growing total populations that later became almost unobtainable? Would you have struggled though the purchase of largely rejected $50 Panama Pacific gold and Indian matte proofs?

If you think the answer to all these questions is yes then you may wish to consider that in order to do so, established collectors at the turn of the last century had to be willing to look at collecting from a relatively new and rapidly evolving perspective. Through out the 1800s collectors by and large recognized date collecting, but not collecting by branch mint. Even as late as 1890 branch mint collecting was still in its infancy and its eventual importance was not yet obvious to the majority. Commemoratives were unheard of. Established "classic" collectors, who began the hobby as children in the 1880s but did not have an open mind, completely missed the 1909-S VDB Lincoln cent, the 1916-D Mercury dime, and the 1921-S Walker among many others.

To the established classic collector, this study poses the question: Are you willing to take the time to stake out the best of the best that the U.S. Mint has to offer in your lifetime? Moderns struck on silver, gold and platinum have massive attractive populations with key dates dramatically rarer than their siblings. These incredibly tight bottlenecks in the series are timeless sign posts of future greatness. Are you willing to look into the probable effects of the dramatic acceleration of design variety showing up in pocket change that has and continues to be the cradle of the next generations collecting habits? To the new collector who would like to expand his interest in coinage beyond 50 states quarters and Presidential dollars, this study is designed to help you understand the nature and potential of the various high-end modern issues so you can pursue your goals with a broader perspective and more confidence.

Those who are concerned about the money creation and high taxation rates required to support the roughly $60 trillion owed to Federal debt holders and pending retirees will appreciate the ultra-long taxable event cycle associated with a high material content rare coin collection. Self-directed IRA holders and estate managers interested in the long-term benefits of numismatics will be able to more effectively allocate family savings.

Coin collecting is a wonderful and enjoyable hobby that builds tangible assets and provides family heirlooms that can be passed down for generations, but in order to consistently select infants bound for greatness you will need to understand the primary market structures that create them and the habits being formed by the new generation of collector.

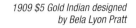
1909 $5 Gold Indian designed by Bela Lyon Pratt

CHAPTER 1

COUNTING THE COST OR 20 YEARS OF WANDERING

Like many coin collectors, I was introduced to the hobby in middle school when my Mom gave me a handful of family coins, and I found it fascinating that some of them were made of silver.

Every Friday the local Planters Bank in my little home town of Waynesboro, Va., was open until 5:30 p.m., so I would hop on my bike and go through rolls of coins for a couple of hours before it closed. Jefferson nickels and Lincoln Memorial cent sets were completed quickly.

Unlike most mature series, our mindset and foresight—not just the strength of our checkbook—determine the quality and potential of our collections.

Every other Saturday I got a special treat. Mom would take me to a coin shop in Staunton, Va., to look through the "junk silver" boxes. To me they were not junk silver at all. They had Walking Liberty halves, Mercury dimes and the occasional worn out Barber quarter that I could never hope to find in the bank rolls.

Robert L., the owner of this little coin shop, was a collector who went into business with his personal collection as his starting inventory. Like so many established collectors, he and some of his regular patrons took an interest in me. ***One older gentleman (who had been working on an outstanding Mercury dime set and a $10 gold Indian set for 40 years) told me something I learned was very important, but that at the time didn't mean that much. He said:***

"I made mistakes early on, I didn't count the cost. Truth is I have never had the money needed to complete the $10 gold set. I should have focused on a gold type set or $5 Indians. I'm glad I got in fairly early on the rarest high grade Mercury's and I should have bought duplicates of the keys while I could still afford them."

Unfortunately this man's wisdom went completely unheeded. Over time I went from collecting easily completed sets to the nearly impossible without thinking about it. Mint State deep cameo proof-like common date Morgan dollars became my first love.

In my late teens I went to work for Larry Pyle at Palmetto Galleries as a coin grader, being ever watchful for affordable proof-like Morgans to add to my collection. As a single college graduate my coin budget expanded dramatically, but my progress on this set started to stall because I didn't need $300 or even $1,000 dollars to make a purchase any more, it was $10,000 -plus, and that is not counting the almost impossible issues from the early to mid-1890s.

Somewhere in the very late 1990s I came to the rational conclusion that if you want to collect attractive high grade classic U.S. coinage, the sets will either tend to be common or almost unobtainable due to sky high key date prices. Furthermore, the value of my collection that now represented a large percentage of my net worth was not doing particularly well when indexed to inflation. Where did I go wrong? Where were the collecting opportunities in my generation to be found? The answer ultimately was found and it was in the same place that the previous generations of coin collectors, who were lucky to be born at the right time, found them. Young, good-looking U.S. Mint series with very scarce affordable key dates have been and continue to be a land of opportunity.

Unlike most mature series, our mindset and foresight—not just the strength of our checkbook—determine the quality and potential of our collections. Two personal experiences illustrate this well. An acquaintance of mine was an avid collector of proof silver Eagles from 1986 until 1995. When the 10th anniversary set came out with the 1995-W proof silver Eagle in it he refused to buy the five-coin set for $1,000 and then sell the four gold Eagles for melt giving him a net cost of $200 for the special issue dollar. The man could afford it but it was an "issue of principle." He felt the Mint had no right to force him to pay 10 times the going rate for a West Point mintmark and saddle him with the inconvenience of having to dump the gold. So, he didn't make the purchase. In the late 1990s the 1995-W silver Eagle was pulling past $1,000 and on its way to over $3,000 by 2008. The frustrated collector sold his incomplete set in disgust.

In the spring of 2005, Lisa Johnson, a customer service representative who worked in the same division as I did, saw a 2004 $25 proof platinum Eagle with the Seated America reverse on my desk and asked about it. I told her that the 2004 platinum quarter was the lowest mintage issue of a rejected series and that the sales for that particular

coin were exceptionally bad because of a recent dramatic spike in the price of platinum. Lisa thought the coin was lovely and was interested in purchasing it if it was rare. Her father ran a store when she was young and gave her quite a few old coins that he picked out of change. She thought the Eagle would be a nice addition to her collection. Lisa was able to come up with the $400 for the 2004 proof platinum eagle quarter and every subsequent year as it came out through 2008. The 2004 and 2008 have already more than doubled in value. When times were good in 2006 and 2007 she worked on the inexpensive back dates and now she has a complete set of proof coins that are rarer on average than the well-respected 1936-1942 proofs. Lisa Johnson is very proud of her set and I suspect she will be more so in 10 years. I'm happy for her.

If we wish to be successful in this "thing we call a hobby" then we need to carefully select series we can afford so our set's progress doesn't stall before we finish it. Learning to spot key coins bound for greatness and developing the confidence to park your money in them early on before the herd shows up is a skill set every collector needs.

The first part of this study is designed to help you graduate from the mere accumulation of coins to focused acquisition of tomorrow's likely numismatic treasures, all the while keeping to a budget.

The second part of this text details how Federal financial misman-agement on an epic scale may make high material content coin collections important family heirlooms that remain resistant to long-term symptoms of rampant indebtedness.

Readers who are wondering if rare, modern U.S. coins are the kind of savings alternative that they have been looking for or are new to numismatics may wish to start with the section entitled "A 60 Trillion Dollar Wind at Your Collection's Back" that begins on page 193 and then come back to the coin related introduction.

CHAPTER 2

CHOOSING OUR COURSE

As we mature in our collecting interest most of us find certain areas of the coin world that we like and specialize in it. While that's completely rational it does beg the question: what areas are we going to spend our time mastering and why? This question is not a new one and collectors who were active from 1906 to 1936 either intentionally or unintentionally made this call. Some stuck with just the "classics" from the 1800s, some focused on just the new material and others pursued some of both. But completely ignoring well-selected "modern" issues

And while we can look through today's coinage books and say that we would have acquired for our collection a 1916-D Mercury dime, a 1916 Standing Liberty quarter, a matte proof gold Indian type set, a matte proof $20 gold Saint-Gaudens, all the key date fractional gold, at least one 1915 Pan Pac $50 commemorative and a 1936 proof set, the likelyhood of us actually having done so if we lived and collected in that era is remote. The reason is every coin listed other than the dime and quarter was an unpopular modern rejected by the collecting public at the time of its issue.

Matte proof gold was expensive and nowhere close to being as impressive as the mirror proofs typical of the late 1800s so they sold very poorly. The incused designs of the $2.50 and $5 gold Indians issued from 1908 to 1929 were not deemed as attractive as the larger gold so they were shunned. The $50 Panama Pacific gold commemoratives had an issue price from the Mint of $100 each. That was an astronomical sum at the time and only about 500 of each were ordered. The king of modern proof sets, the 1936 issue, came out in the midst of the commemorative mania. Commemorative halves in every imaginable variety were flying out of the Mint in 1936 and not even one of them turned out to be a serious coin, but the over looked 1936 proof set with its tiny 3,800 mintage proved to be outstanding.

It is often said that the past is a prelude to the future and there are very few arenas where that is truer than the coin world. Successful modern collectors at that time:

1. Made early purchases of rejected low population coins with many siblings while they were still cheap because they realized the set drives the keys.

2. Ignored the temptation to chase the herd and its high mintage fads.

3. Allowed the new collecting masses to tip them off to the fact that the way sets were being put together were not going to be just date-based series anymore. The date and mintmark collecting era was upon them.

We need to master precisely the same skill set. ***In order to consistently select today's modern coins bound for greatness we first need to understand the primary market structures that make them special and the habits being formed by the new generation of collector.*** Let's start with the basics.

Forms of Collecting:

Most successful collections are built around structures There are two primary and two subordinate forms:

1. SERIES DATE AND MINTMARK COLLECTING. A collector acquires one of every date and mintmark ever produced for a particular coin. Normally that means that every coin looks identical except for some minor differentiating mark, typically a date or mintmark showing where and when the coin was struck.

2. TYPE COLLECTING. A collector acquires by design, denomination or composition normally in proof or mint state form. For example, a silver proof half collector would want a single proof example of at least one Seated Liberty, Barber, Walking Liberty, Franklin and Kennedy half for his collection to be complete. Every mirror proof half in this example has a profoundly different design.

A mint state Barber type set would consist of a Barber dime, Barber quarter and Barber half. In this case the design is the same but each denomination must be present.

Barber Coins

A Lincoln cent type collector would likely want at a minimum the eight issues pictured below. They have a common image of Lincoln on the obverse but the reverse has seen multiple designs over the years. Notice also that the 1943 "steel" cent has a drastically different appearance than its copper colored siblings.

Lincoln Cents

3. DIE VARIETY COLLECTING. A collector builds a collection around noticeable differences in coins of the same series that may have the same date and mintmark. An example of this could be inscriptions with different fonts, corrected mintmarks or slight variations of die images. This form of coinage differentiation is not considered as strong or as cohesive as the two dominant collecting structures.

4. FREE-FORM COLLECTING. A collector chooses coins that are considered outstanding or enjoyed for some personal reason. They tend be comprised of keys to major series in high grade or ultra-low mintage type coins. The rarity collector or speculator frequently practices this form of holding coins.

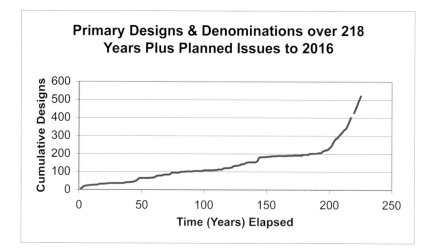

Primary Designs & Denominations over 218 Years Plus Planned Issues to 2016

Primary Design Change Rates Since 1793

The U.S. Mint opened its doors for business in 1793 and by 1809 had already developed and produced more than 30 coins with completely different designs and denominations. After that stagnation set in until the 1828-1840 period, when the Mint was developing on average more than one new coin a year. In 1837 the Mint introduced *the Seated Liberty design that would dominate* silver half dimes, dimes, quarters, halves and dollars in one form or another *for the next 54 years.*

Liberty Head gold came into production in 1838 and remained fundamentally unchanged on the quarter eagle, half eagle, eagle and double eagle until it went out of service completely in 1908. *"Unified designs" and "sameness" were the policy of the day and it had direct consequences for those who took an interest in collecting U.S. coinage.*

Large cents and half cents production was suspended in 1857 and the nostalgic American public began putting together date sets from pocket change. Coin collecting took off and continued to grow along with the public's disposable income in an uneven manner from then on. If you wished to collect silver or gold coinage from pocket change from the 1840s to the early 1890s your choices were quite limited. Through out the 1800s up until the late 1880s collecting by mintmarks was not an established collecting form.

But a few pioneers recognized that collecting by date and by mintmark would dramatically increase their collecting options. In the early 1890s a text promoting series collecting by branch mint came to market. *Series date and mintmark collecting, which would much later become the primary U.S. coin collecting form, was born although not quickly adopted.*

Roosevelt Inaugural Medal

The tradition of incredibly long running designs was canonized in 1890 when Congress enacted legislation requiring at least 25 years to pass between design changes for each denomination. Unfortunately this locked in designs that were held in contempt by the artistic community, the public and even top political figures. The dissatisfaction came to a head when Teddy Roosevelt notified the Secretary of the Treasury that our coinage was of "atrocious hideousness."

Roosevelt's very impressive inaugural medal was designed by the incredibly talented sculptor Augustus Saint-Gaudens, so he was commissioned to start the task of redesigning our gold using allegorical images reminiscent of ancient Greek coinage. Between 1907 and 1916, Saint-Gaudens and his peers issued in a "golden age" of artistic excellence. This brief period was a once-in-a-lifetime opportunity that produced the Lincoln cent, Buffalo nickel, Mercury dime, Standing Liberty quarter, Walking Liberty half, three Indian gold fractionals, the Saint-Gaudens double eagle and the Panama-Pacific commemoratives. Good new designs were on the move, and it was exciting. *Those who started working on complete date and mintmark sets while they were still in their infancy were well rewarded for their foresight.*

It's nothing short of amazing that most collectors at the time largely overlooked design and denomination type coin rarities with mintages that had not been seen since the 1860s and would not be approached again for about 100 years. Expensive large denomination gold type coins sold to the public at a premium – like the matte proof quarter eagle, half eagle, eagle and double eagle – were largely rejected by the collecting public. The Panama-Pacific Mint State $50 gold commemoratives only sold about half of their miniscule 1,000 coin authorized striking run. *So much for the foresight of the collecting establishment*

that was unwilling to pay a premium for new special issues! These coins are all selling for $12,000 to $80,000 apiece now.

In the mid-1930s series date and mintmark coinage boards and holders came out for the very popular contemporary circulating coins that could still be found in pocket change. This relatively design-rich period culminated in the 1930s commemorative boom. From 1907 to 1939 more than 50 new designs and denominations were introduced, with 21 of those being commemoratives for sale in 1936 alone!

Abuses in the commemorative program prompted Congress to suspend authorization of new commemorative coins in 1937, thus returning to an unbelievably long period of design stability. Lincoln cents, Jefferson nickels, Roosevelt dimes and Washington quarters collected by date and mintmark were practically the only option available for collectors looking through pocket change.

The Mint is fully aware that design changes encourage collecting by roll or "hoarding" of U.S. coinage, which is why only about 60 different fundamental circulating designs and denominations graced U.S. coinage from 1809 to 1964. These policies in turn impacted collector habits and ultimately the pricing structures for the U.S. coin markets. ***This period of design stability is over.***

As you can see from the previous chart, ***design change has gone almost hyperbolic***. With the introduction of the eagles program and the return of commemoratives in the mid-1980s something other than the same old designs were available again even if it was mostly found on precious metal issues. Then came real game changer – stable obverse and changing reverse series intended for circulation. Let's look at them:

- Fifty States Quarters
- United States Territories Quarters
- National Parks Quarters
- Westward Journey Nickels
- Sacagawea Native American Dollars Series
- Presidential Dollars
- Life of Lincoln Cents

Notice that these seven programs alone will represent 180 new designs in roughly 20 years. That's three times as many as in the last 200 years!

The reason why what is in circulation is more important than obsolete precious metal series or precious metal moderns is that they are silent advertisements for coin collecting that are seen every day by almost every citizen on a constant basis. That kind of market exposure is priceless and it's where most people start the hobby. According to the U.S. Mint, there are roughly 100,000,000 people collecting the changing reverse series in various forms. This next generation of collector is forming their habits now and they are being trained by the Mint to expect a high degree of design variation in their sets. *Most of the world has thousands of years of coinage history and thousands of designs to draw from, so they tend to emphasize type collecting over series date and mintmarks because they can.*

Just as we look back on the 1907-1916 era as "The Golden Age" of outstanding artistic merit, the period we are in now may be looked back on as the dawn of "The Great Type Series." *The U.S. has entered a new design-based era.* It's important that this process work for us, not against us and that we understand to the fullest extent possible how series behave over time.

CHAPTER 4

RARE COIN MARKET BEHAVIOR

Stable Series Pricing Models
and the Importance of Relative Rarity

Until recently almost all U.S. series except for the classic
commemoratives have enjoyed amazingly predictable pricing
structures that flow from their constant series designs. In
order to understand the long term price behavior associated
with rare coins, it's necessary to examine series with mature
pricing structures and mintage or surviving population tables
that are representative of the number of coins still available to

Let's start with the proof Walking Liberty halves issued from 1936 to 1942. *For a detailed graph description and ratio definitions, see Appendix A.*

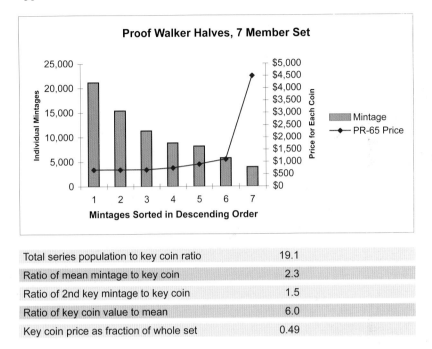

Proof Walker Halves, 7 Member Set

Total series population to key coin ratio	19.1
Ratio of mean mintage to key coin	2.3
Ratio of 2nd key mintage to key coin	1.5
Ratio of key coin value to mean	6.0
Key coin price as fraction of whole set	0.49

The relative rarity price curve is a good representation of a classic demand curve in economics and more importantly it *is highly inelastic and kinked for the key date*. This behavior makes perfect sense. For the sake of simplicity let's assume there are 6,000 series collectors seeking to complete a seven-year proof Walking Liberty date set. Any years with mintages above 6,000 result in a surplus of coins on the market. These excess coins will never be part of a complete set, so their value is determined primarily by those seeking a representative example of the proof Walker series.

Regardless of whether the "surplus" available is 2,000 coins or 10,000, these are type coins and the market assigns their value accordingly. Among the Walking Liberty proof halves, a 60 percent decrease in mintage results in only a 30 percent increase in sales price between the most common and the third rarest coin in the series. The second rarest issue has a mintage of 5,700, so in our example there would be 300 collectors who will never be able to acquire one. This creates competition for available coins, with a resulting upward pressure on the sales price. A 30 percent decrease in mintage (supply) results in a 25 percent increase in price between the second and third rarest issues. This is where the fireworks start. In our example, we would have 5,700 collectors who could obtain every year except the key date, which has a mintage of only 3,900. The 31 percent reduction in mintage between 1936 and 1937 produces a four-fold increase in sales price. The number of complete Walking Liberty half proof sets that can be assembled is limited by the number of 1936 halves. Thus the rarest coin in each set is referred to as the "key" to the set.

Indian Head $2.5 Gold

Similar pricing behavior takes place in uncirculated MS-60 $2.5 gold Indians from 1908 to 1929.

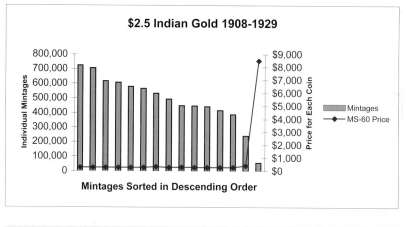

Total Series population to key coin ratio	131.00
Ratio of Mean mintage to key coin	8.80
Ratio of Second key to key mintage	4.30
Ratio of key coin value to mean	31.00
Key coins price as fraction of set	0.68

Since the population of $2.5 Indian gold coins was originally intended for circulation, a large percentage were circulated to some degree, but certainly not to the extent of the majority of smaller denomination silver coins of the period. Population reports from NGC and PCGS indicate that the current relative population relationships are fundamentally still valid.

The mintage of the 1911-D is less than one-quarter of the next rarest coin in the series. *The relatively large total mintage of the common dates places tremendous pressure on this key date. Indeed, the relative rarity of the 1911-D key is profound. The ratio of the key coin value to the typical mint state $2.5 Indian is approximately 31 to 1.* The key date 1936 Walking Liberty proof half has a much lower actual mintage, and fewer of them show up in NGC and PCGS population reports, but the 1911-D $2.5 Indian gold coin commands significantly higher prices, even when one takes into account the higher bullion value.

The very important and predictable phenomenon of relative rarity in stable design series is played out convincingly with proof Walking Liberty silver $1 Eagles issued from 1986 to present.

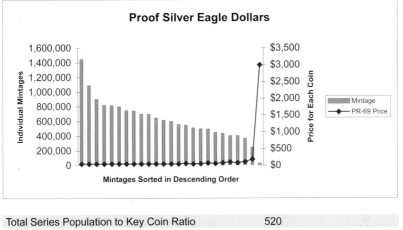

Total Series Population to Key Coin Ratio	520
Ratio of Mean Mintage to Key Coin Ratio	20
Ratio of 2nd Key Mintage to Key Coin	8.3
Ratio of Key Coin Value to Mean	66
Key Coin Price as Fraction of Whole Set	0.67

Notice that the key to this series – the 1995-W—is NOT rare. The 1995-W has a total mintage of over 30,000, and virtually every one of those coins still exists in a collectible grade.

1986 Silver Eagle

The 1995-W proof silver Eagle key is about eight times more common than the key 1936 proof Walking Liberty half, but commands almost the same price depending on grade. These coins have similar designs and are struck on the same metal. *The 1995-W is eight times rarer than any other coin in the proof silver Eagle series, and there are over 15 million common dates in the marketplace, which builds a large collector base for the key coin. This relative bottleneck in the series is profound, and is reflected in the fact that the key trades at 60 times the price of the typical proof silver Eagle.* This coin's price may reflect near maturity already.

Some rare coin investment advisers suggest that modern U.S. coins struck on gold, silver or platinum are a poor investment because too many high grade examples are present in the market. *Large quantities of common date high grade material in a series that is collected by date and mintmark are a blessing,* whether one is talking about a modern coin or a 100-year-old Morgan dollar, *because a large quantity of attractive and affordable common date coins are essentially advertisements for the series keys.* The real question to be considered is how many of those keys are available and how much collector base compression will be generated.

Series with stable designs whose primary form of differentiation between issues is just a date and mintmark are fairly straightforward in price behavior. Series keys essentially occupy bottlenecks in the larger series populations and relative rarity among members along with the popularity of the set dictates values. Coins that lack identical design elements that enforce set cohesion are dramatically more difficult to model and predict.

Unstable Design Models and
Type Coin Market Dynamics

When coinage series do not have some strong form of design and denominational unity the relative rarity models break down. Values are determined to a large extent by design appeal and not rarity. Notice that the pricing stability associated with the stable design relative rarity model based on dates and mintmarks is completely gone.

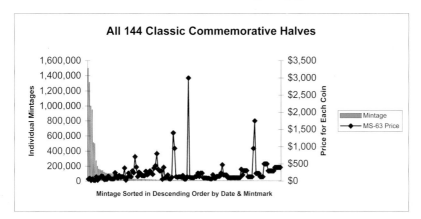

How can this happen? Well, the answer is found in these comments made by a very experienced and competent commemorative collector named Marbella on the PCGS coin boards:

"It's kind of hard being a commemorative collector, because you have to make your own rules. It is insane to do the whole 144-piece set. Even the 50-piece type set seems crazy given that some of the designs are hideous (Wisconsin) and some "events" are ridiculous (Cincinnati

Wisconsin
Territorial
Centennial

*Cincinnati
Music Center*

*Music Center). Oregon is beautiful and everyone with an interest in
commems wants one. So everyone decides what they want, what they
like, what is relevant to them, and buys that."*

**Looking at the total mintages of each design vs. price gives a
much better picture of what is going on.**

Commemorative silver half dollars issued 1892 to 1954 offer a
wealth of information that's useful to us, as do the commemorative
silver dollars issued from 1983 to present. Let's look at some examples:

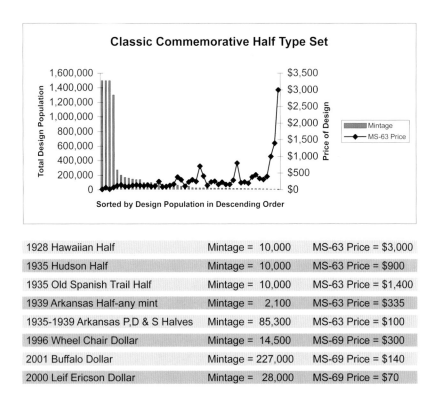

1928 Hawaiian Half	Mintage = 10,000	MS-63 Price = $3,000
1935 Hudson Half	Mintage = 10,000	MS-63 Price = $900
1935 Old Spanish Trail Half	Mintage = 10,000	MS-63 Price = $1,400
1939 Arkansas Half-any mint	Mintage = 2,100	MS-63 Price = $335
1935-1939 Arkansas P,D & S Halves	Mintage = 85,300	MS-63 Price = $100
1996 Wheel Chair Dollar	Mintage = 14,500	MS-69 Price = $300
2001 Buffalo Dollar	Mintage = 227,000	MS-69 Price = $140
2000 Leif Ericson Dollar	Mintage = 28,000	MS-69 Price = $70

The Hawaiian, Hudson and Old Spanish Trail halves all possess the same basic rarity, but the Hawaiian design is popular and sought after while the Hudson and Spanish Trail designs are less so resulting in a three-fold price difference. As of this writing the Buffalo dollar ranks close to last in terms of rarity in the modern mint state commemorative silver dollar type set, but it's the sixth most expensive because it has unreal design appeal. The Ericson dollar is eight times rarer than the Buffalo dollar, but it trades for half the price.

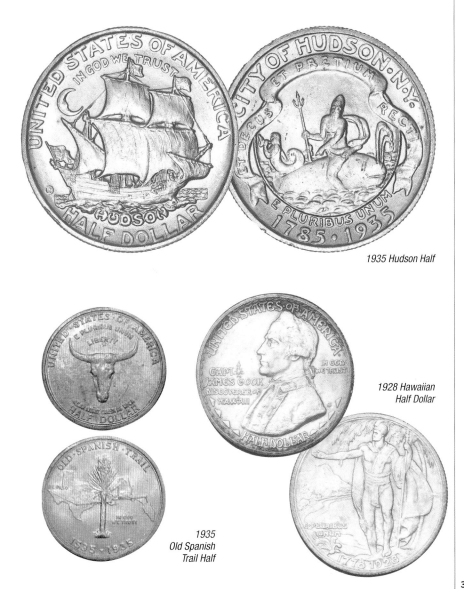

1935 Hudson Half

*1928 Hawaiian
Half Dollar*

*1935
Old Spanish
Trail Half*

Notice the Arkansas halves are a 15-coin series with a 85,000 total population whose key dates are ultra low mintage but it does not matter. The set is collected by design not date and mintmark, so a 2,100 mintage coin is "seen" by the market as one of 85,000 coins with a pair of native Americans on the front of which only 10,000 are needed to complete someone's type set. This same process plays out over and over again with the Oregon Trail, Daniel Boone, Texas and Booker T. Washington sets. The sets are fairly large and the keys are date and mintmark rare but they are regarded as common because they are judged based on the rarity of the design not date and mintmark.

Important Ramifications:

1. *Coins without design cohesion are stand-alone issues and the market prices them accordingly.*
2. *You don't want a series you collect by date and mintmark to become collected by type because it undermines the value of the key dates.*
3. *When a series is comprised of many different designs without clearly unifying design elements the series will likely be collected by design type.*

Daniel Boone Bicentennial

Booker T. Washington

Oregon Trail Memorial

Texas Centennial

The Dawn of Changing Reverse Series

The U.S. Mint is well aware that new designs increase collector interest and result in what they call an "inaugural sales spike" in the first year or first few years of issue. Starting in late the1990s, the Mint started looking at a new series structure for its coins incorporating a stable obverse and a changing reverse. The 50 State quarters is the largest and most famous example of this up and coming structure. The stable obverse of George Washington enforces a strict relative rarity pricing structure and gives the series much needed cohesion that earlier type coins and commemoratives lacked. Design variation that keep the coins interesting without the problems normally associated with collecting by type is a wonderful new development.

Let's look at the price and mintage profile of every silver proof quarter from 1950 to 2008 including the 10-year 50 State quarters program.

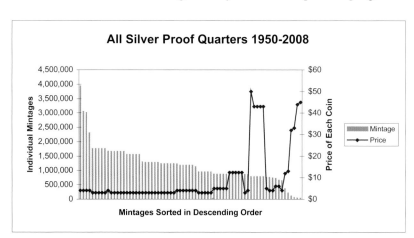

Introducing changing designs into a long running stable design series modifies the relationships between series date and mintmark rarity and price behavior. The 1999 silver state proof quarters with an 800,000 mintage are worth about the same as the 1950 silver proof quarters with a 50,000 mintage! Why is the market behaving this way? There are 25 million Washington silver proof quarters with an eagle on the reverse and just 800,000 1999 silver Washington proof quarters with states on the reverse. The 1999 silver quarters rule the type set while the 1950 quarter is king of the 1950-1998 date set.

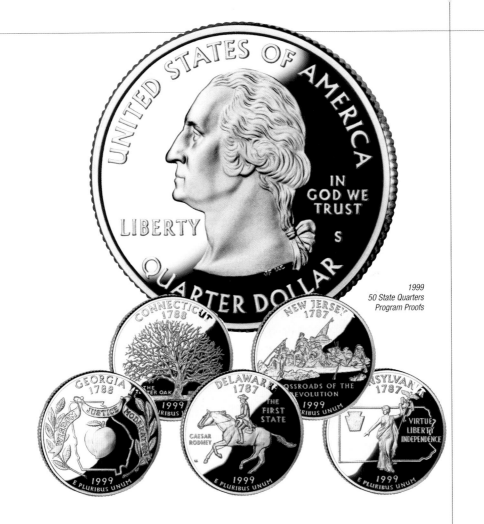

The strength of the changing reverse type set is stunning. The 1999 silver proof quarters alone have a total market value of around 180 million dollars. The total market value of all silver proof quarters combined from 1936 to 1998 with an eagle on the reverse is roughly 130 million.

It is a common belief that the 50 State quarters energized the collector base for the previously stagnant Washington quarter series but this is only partially true. The lead coins to the entire silver proof Washington quarter set are the 1936-1942 and the 1950-1954 issues, so if the 50 State silver proof quarters collectors migrated in significant numbers to the earlier coins and started collecting by date it should show up in the early coins values indexed to constant dollars but that's not what the data indicates.

Proof Washington Quarter Prices
Indexed to Inflation & Stated in 2008 Dollars

YEAR	SERIES	CONSTANT DOLLAR SET VALUE
2008	1936-1942 Proof Set in PR-64	$2,500
1988	1936-1942 Proof Set in PR-64	$3,000
1968	1936-1942 Proof Set in PR-64	$2,600
2008	1950-1954 Proof Short Set in PR-64	$300
1988	1950-1954 Proof Short Set in PR-64	$600
1968	1950-1954 Proof Short Set in PR-64	$475

Remember these pre-1955 proof coins have tiny date-based mintages compared to their 50 state silver siblings. There are hundreds of thousands of 50 State silver proof quarter collectors and if there was a significant migration from the changing reverse issues collector base into the date-based portion of the series the results should have been phenomenal but they weren't. There are only about 4,000 1936 proof quarters around. More or less *1 percent of the collector base for the States program would wipe out the entire existing population of 1936 issues forcing prices up to the point that some of the previous holders sold. Prices for early proof Washingtons should be at an inflation adjusted all-time high but they are not. The proof State quarter collector base is making its true preferences known.*

The impression that the mint state issue 50 State quarters helped the classic mint state set is partially justified. The Mint says there are close to 100 million 50 State quarter collectors and it looks like there are only about 2,000 1932-D mint state quarters and 4,000 mint state 1932-S pieces and they both have a grading bell line center of MS-62. *So if just one out of every 50,000 state quarters collectors decided to take up collecting the early dates in any mint state grade it should absorb the entire population of keys and drive the real term price hyperbolic, but it didn't.*

1950 Washington Quarter

2009
U.S. Territories
Quarters Program

Year	Early Key Date Quarters-2008 Constant Dollars	MS-60	MS-63
2008	1932D Mint State Quarter	$775	$2,600
1988	1932D Mint State Quarter	$610	$1,100
1968	1932D Average BU (MS-62) was $1,400	1000 est.	$1,600 est

Year	Early Key Date Quarters-2008 Constant Dollars	MS-60	MS-63
2008	1932S Mint State Quarter	$390	$900
1988	1932S Mint State Quarter	$350	$600
1968	1932S Average BU (MS-62) was $720	$500 est.	$800 est.

Year	Early Key Date Quarters-2008 Constant Dollars	MS-60	MS-63
2008	1936D Mint State Quarter	$475	$750
1988	1936D Mint State Quarter	$350	$500
1968	1936D Average BU (MS-62) was $600	$500 est.	$650 est.

Quarter prices are reprinted with permission from the Coin Dealer Newsletter, POB 7939, Torrance CA 90504, www.graysheet.com
Copyright CDN Inc. 2010

Merging Stable Design Date and Mintmark Series with New Changing Reverse Sets

1. *Most new changing reverse series collectors do not in fact migrate to include the older static designs in their sets. The older coins are just a single type coin to them.*

2. A tiny fraction of the changing reverse collectors will go on to collect the stable back dates but the number of new changing reverse entrants needs to be staggering and the old key dates very rare in order to have any chance of creating net inflation adjusted growth on the old sets.

3. Those new entrants who do bother to go back and pick up the early coins tend to focus on the very finest and rarest early issues. *Notice that MS-60 coins, regardless of their status as a key or semi key, have displayed zero real term growth in 40 years. Semi keys have*

languished in real terms. The early 1936-1942 silver proof quarters have shown zero real term growth in 40 years. The greatest of all early keys the 1932-D has been able to buck the trend in higher grades and show appreciable real term value growth in the last 10 to 20 years and it probably is 50 State quarters induced.

4. Washington quarters have seen days of growth and glory but they were in the first 30 years of the maturation process. These early 1932 mint state and 1936 proof keys moved from less than $10 each in today's dollars to $500 - $1,500 each by the time they were 30 years old! That's an "energized collector base."

This behavior could show up in any stable design series currently in production for a number of years that later goes to a changing reverse. We know for a fact the Sacagawea dollar is facing this structure and Congress was taught a valuable lesson in 2007 by the convergence of the Sacagawea and Presidential dollars programs.

Sacagawea Dollar with Changing Reverse

Competition Among Series With Different Structures

The Mint and its allies in Congress are fully aware that the best place to look for collector base growth is the collector series with changing reverses. In the fact finding section of the Presidential Dollar Law known as Public Law 109-145 section 101 (3) it is stated:

The success of the 50 States quarter program "shows that a design on a United States circulating coin that is regularly changed in a manner *similar to the systematic change in design in such program radically increases demand for the coin.*"

For political reasons, the same law required that the Mint produce the stable reverse designed Sacagawea dollar at the same time as the changing obverse Presidential series was running. The law states:

"The Secretary annually shall mint and issue such Sacagawea Design $1 coins for circulation in quantities of no less than 1/3 of the total $1 coins minted and issued under this subsection."

The stable theme "Sacagawea" dollars have effectively been placed in direct competition for public demand with a changing obverse dollar series and the results were obvious. The Sacagawea dollars started pilling up in government vaults. About a year later, in order to make the "Sac" dollar competitive, Congress instructed the Secretary to use on the reverse:

"Images celebrating the important contributions made by Indian Tribes and individual Native Americans to the development of the united States and the history of the United States."

There are many variables like price, size, material content, total population, age and beauty that impact collector interest in any given series but one thing is clear; if two series are competing in the same market segment for new converts the changing reverse series has a distinct advantage.

Now that we have set the groundwork for series structures let's look at how their key dates are created and appreciate over time.

1915 Panama
Pacific $50 Gold
Commemoratives

The "stone rejected by the builders" will become the "chief cornerstone" regardless of whether the majority recognizes it at the time or not.

CHAPTER 5

KEYS IN THEIR INFANCY

Almost without exception the most sought after coins (most expensive) had something go wrong or were rejected for some reason in their year of production or soon thereafter. These are the coins that must be identified early in the process by the collector who does not want to pay an exorbitant penalty for a lack of foresight. Let's take a walk through coinage history for some excellent examples of what creates great coins.

TOO EXPENSIVE: The 1915 Panama Pacific $50 gold commemoratives were $100 each. Final sales didn't even come close to maximum allowed mintages and they are $35,000 -$125,000 each today. The 1928 Hawaiian commemorative half dollar was sold at four times its face value at the time of its issue. This was the highest premium up to this time. The Hawaiian is now one of the greatest of the classic commemoratives and carries a $2,000-5000 price tag to go with it. The 1995-W proof Walking Liberty silver Eagle (dollar) was only available in a five-coin set with a price tag of $1,000. If the set had been purchased and the gold coins sold at melt the net cost to the purchaser for the dollar was about $200. The 1995-W currently trades for roughly $3,000.

DILUTION OF COLLECTOR DEMAND: In the two-year period from 1995-1996 the Mint issued 12 different silver commemorative dollars. Total collector demand had become so fractured that in 1996 mintages fell by as much as 70 percent off the previous modern commemorative dollar low creating the five lowest mintage dollars of the entire 50-plus type coin program. What cost about $150 for five coins in 1996 is now over $1,400.

TOO UGLY: Collectors making purchases tend to gravitate to attractive coinage, which is completely understandable. Coins with little artistic merit do come to market from time to time for politically motivated reasons and they don't sell well contributing to the creation of profound relative rarities. There have been several excellent examples of this in the last 20 years. The coins are trading at 10 times their issue price, but the names of the coins will not be mentioned to protect the guilty.

PRODUCTION RUN CUT SHORT: Coins that have a very short production period for whatever reason are going to be significantly rarer, all else being equal. A good example of this is the 1916 Standing Liberty quarter, whose production started very late in the year. Its original mintage was only 52,000 and the coin has a current market price of over $15,000 in mint state grades.

1916 Standing Liberty Quarter

1933 $20 Saint-Gaudens
Gold Double Eagle

MASS MELTING OF COINAGE: The ever famous 1933 $20 Saint-Gaudens gold double eagles and the 1933 $10 Indian gold eagles had almost their entire populations wiped out in massive coinage melts brought on by the Great Depression.

NOT SAVED FROM CIRCULATION: The1932-S Washington quarter has the lowest mintage of all the mint state early issues of 408,000. Its sibling, the 1932-D, was second place at 436,800. This was widely known at the time and as a result more of the 1932-S issues were saved. Now the 1932-D trades for two to three times as much as the 1932-S in typical mint state grades. A MS-63 1932-D brings approximately $2,500 today.

BLANK SHORTAGE: Shortages in physical material obviously limit production capacity and this impacted the 2008 and 2009 special issue production runs in a profound way.

TOO HARD TO STRIKE: The 1907 high relief $20 Saint-Gaudens double eagle was discontinued by the Mint because its very high relief required entirely too much time and effort for a production coin and so only 11,250 were created. Most are over $10,000 now.

RECESSION INDUCED BACKFLOW TO THE FEDERAL RESERVE: Pocket change that sits around in containers in the public's homes has the tendency to be placed in rolls and returned to the banks in times of economic difficulty. A Federal Reserve with more coins than it knows what to do with doesn't order coins from the Mint and mintages can free fall. This is what we are seeing in 2008 to present. Below is what happened to combined production from all mints (P, D and S) from 1928 to 1935 for precisely this reason.

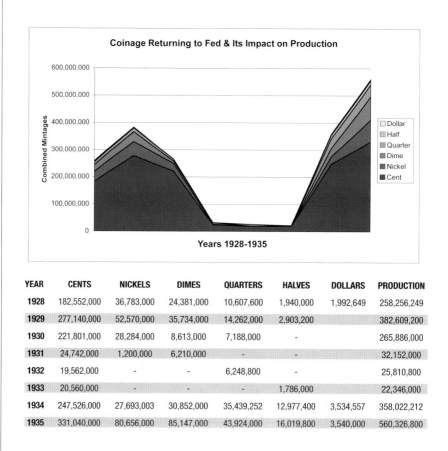

Coinage Returning to Fed & Its Impact on Production

YEAR	CENTS	NICKELS	DIMES	QUARTERS	HALVES	DOLLARS	PRODUCTION
1928	182,552,000	36,783,000	24,381,000	10,607,600	1,940,000	1,992,649	258,256,249
1929	277,140,000	52,570,000	35,734,000	14,262,000	2,903,200		382,609,200
1930	221,801,000	28,284,000	8,613,000	7,188,000	-		265,886,000
1931	24,742,000	1,200,000	6,210,000	-	-		32,152,000
1932	19,562,000	-	-	6,248,800	-		25,810,800
1933	20,560,000	-	-	-	1,786,000		22,346,000
1934	247,526,000	27,693,003	30,852,000	35,439,252	12,977,400	3,534,557	358,022,212
1935	331,040,000	80,656,000	85,147,000	43,924,000	16,019,800	3,540,000	560,326,800

In the end, it doesn't matter which reason or combination of reasons creates the rarity. Rejection by the Mint or the contemporary collectors of an issue that is a member of a significant U.S. series is a formula for excellent price growth even if it takes five to 10 years for it to materialize. *The "stone rejected by the builders" will become the "chief cornerstone" regardless of whether the majority recognizes it at the time or not.*

The best way to watch for this is to subscribe to coin magazines like Numismatic News that do a good job of keeping their readers up on the latest U.S. Mint weekly sales reports. If a coin looks like its going to be the rarest of its series regardless of the reason or a type coin with a final mintage of 2,000 – 6,000 it should be seriously considered because it's breaking into either key coin status or 100-year type rarity.

Time, Inventory and Price – Reaching Maturity

When a modern coin sells out at a very low mintage in a popular series the market will normally follow a very predictable behavior pattern as shown below.

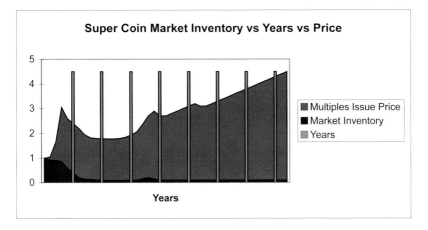

It all starts when a coin goes to back order or no longer available at the Mint unexpectedly resulting in a very low final number. Immediately after the sellout there will still be a few available at a fraction over issue price on various 24-hour Web sites. This is a fleeting opportunity to buy from dealers who aren't paying close attention.

As the news of a major mintage anomaly spreads, many dealers and flippers holding inventory momentarily stop selling. At the same time, demand is materializing due to widening market realization and the combination produces the sharp upward price spike. Normally somewhere between two and four times issue price the dealers and flippers start dumping in mass and the prices start dropping. This initial spike and retraction process takes about one to two years. The trough typically bottoms out about 30 to 40 percent off the year-one highs and stays flat for a couple years while the remaining market inventory "finds homes." The long-term climb stage has now been set. Notice how the small bump in dealer inventory created by a marketer taking a position after the material has dispersed creates a pronounced price spike because the market is so thin after year three.

The moral of this story is if a coin you need for your collection goes "no longer available" with an exceedingly low mintage act quickly and buy it on the after market and don't let a fractional price increase of 25 to 50 percent bother you. Two to four times issue price is coming soon. If you miss this brief aftermarket window, patience may be needed.

Inaugural Spikes—The Keys Normally Come Later

The boost in sales enjoyed by new series is frequently referred to as an inaugural spike.

These charts illustrate the phenomenon. The first chart is a composite sales profile of 10 modern series that have run for at least 12 years and whose first year of sales was not abbreviated for some reason. The second chart represents four series whose first year of issue was abnormally short.

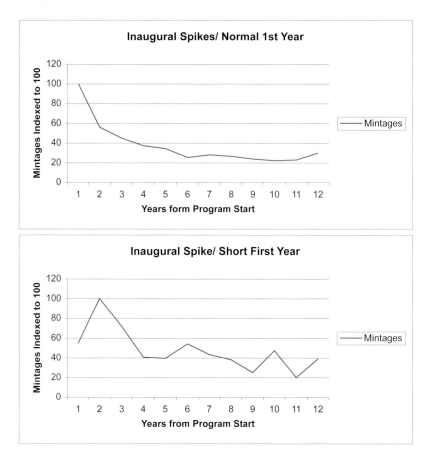

MODERN COMMEMORATIVE COINS

There are a couple of things we can take away from the data.

1. The public likes new programs and once the initial rush to acquire is over sales drop dramatically and tend to bottom out somewhere after the fourth year of issue.

2. If you have a limited collecting budget and can't momentarily afford all the series you wish to pursue, in most cases it's best to focus your expenditures on the more established series that is in the trough than the new series whose mintages are likely to drop.

Series Life Cycles and Growth Rates

When series are in their infancy their key dates have not "stretched out" from the prices of the common dates in a meaningful way. Inventory in the market is as large as its ever going to be and the collector base has not had the opportunity to grow. The time to put together a serious set is while the coins are being produced or right after the series goes obsolete. And be very picky about the quality of each coin while you are at it. These great classic series illustrate the point:

	Complete Set Price	Value First 4 Keys	Intrinsic Value
Mercury Dimes MS-63	$26,000	$19,000	$100
Walker Halves MS-63	$102,000	$58,000	$400
$2.5 Gold Indians MS-63	$35,000	$24,000	$2,000
$5 Gold Indians MS-63	$210,000	$140,000	$5,000
$20 Gold Saints MS-63	$2,500,000+	$2,000,000+	$50,000

Notice that over half the entire series value is contained in the first four keys at the time of series maturity. This is why so many authors of coin books correctly stress the importance of key dates in high grade. But what they don't often stress is the importance of making your purchases while the series and its keys are still in their infancy and relatively close to intrinsic value.

If you were a collector from 1906 to 1945 the best course of action would have been to focus your efforts on the very best contemporary coinage you could find while it was still available. In general the growth of mature series is nothing like as great as it is earlier in its maturation cycle.

Coins and their series go through a maturity process like everything else worth owning. Economist and marketing people have attempted to describe and quantify this development process and tailor it to fit the their niche but they are all trying to describe the same basic behavior.

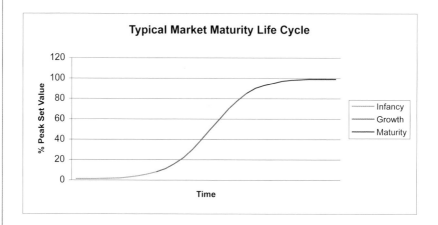

There is a reason that coins issued prior to the World War II are not appreciating the way they used to on a constant dollar percentage basis. They are all over 50 years old now, and they are well into the maturity phase of the life cycle.

Thankfully most modern series issued since 1986 are in the late infancy stage. Issues like proof silver Eagles and $5 mint state gold commemoratives are already into the mid to late growth phase and their keys are about to cool off on a percentage basis.

Long-Term Growth Rates Among Denominations

Prior to the First World War small fractional gold series were more widely collected than their larger counterparts because among other things the US general population had not seen enough growth in disposable income to carry the cost of the high denomination sets. We can expect US disposable income behavior over the next 20 years to impact interdenominational key date performance. Lower real wages favor smaller denominations.

There are many unified designs with multiple denominations among the ranks of both classic and modern coinage. In most cases the smallest denominations have higher populations than the physically larger coins and the larger issues are more impressive. If you want the big coins and can afford them then by all means pick them up, but if you cannot then don't feel like you compromised because of budget constraints. *On a percentage basis, David normally slays Goliath as long as they are both struck on the same metal.* Note that doubling the denomination only produces about a 50 percent increase in mature market value in most cases except where condition rarity in higher grades skews the figures as is seen in the $20 Liberty. This listing shows mostly unified designs in multiple denominations.

Unified Designs	Population	PR-64 Price
$2.5 Indian Matte Proof Gold Eagle	1,400	$12,000
$5 Indian Matte Proof Gold Eagle	700	$15,000
$10 Indian Matte Proof Gold Eagle	600	$20,000
$20 Saint Gaudens Matte Proof Gold	500	$30,000
Barber Dime Proof	13,000	$800
Barber Quarter Proof	12,000	$1,200
Barber Half Proof	13,000	$1,500
$2.5 Liberty Head Proof Gold	3,000	$7,000
$5 Liberty Gold Proof with Motto	2,200	$13,000
$10 Liberty Gold Proof with Motto	1,700	$17,000
$20 Liberty Gold Proof with Motto	1,800	$36,000
Seated Dime Proof with Legend	20,000	$800
Seated Quarter Proof with Motto	18,000	$1,300
Seated Half Proof with Motto	17,000	$1,800

$20 Coronet Head Gold Eagle Type III

CHAPTER 6

MODERNS AS DESIGN AND DENOMINATION BASED TYPE RARITIES

Some classic collectors would suggest that a modern coin with the same obverse and annually changing reverse does not constitute a distinct type coin worthy of separate listing in a type coin ranking. There are numerous examples of classic coinage that have long been counted as distinct types that have stable obverse designs and precious little reverse design change. For example, $20 Coronet Head gold eagles are described as Type I, Type II or Type III based on primarily the presence or absence of the motto "In God

$20 Coronet Head gold eagle Type I

We Trust" on the reverse or the presence of the word "Dollars." Its smaller sibling, the $5 Coronet gold, also enjoys multiple type status for the same reason. So in this case, five denominations with the same primary obverse design and a few minor reverse changes constitute about 10 separate antique gold type coins. Type coin rarity is defined in terms of how many coins exist of each design, denomination and composition regardless of whether they are new or old.

$2.5 Liberty Head Proof Gold

We collect coins because they have what marketing people call product differentiation. Obviously design change is a more profound form of differentiation than just changing a design trivial mark like a date, mintmark or star. Let's look at a listing of the rarest design and denomination-based mint state type coins issued to the general public in the last 200 years. Coins only available to dignitaries and special institutions are not included. These listings are a compilation of the estimated surviving populations of design and denomination based rare coins in Mint State 60 (MS-60) or better grades. Classics grading almost uncirculated (AU-58) and lower are not included in the listed populations even though they are still in many cases very attractive coins. **Classics are in black** and **moderns are in red**.

These listings are not intended to be exact, nor indeed can they be. They are a composite of long established mintage tables pulled from *U.S. Coin Digest*, the NGC and PCGS combined population reports, various writings by Q. David Bowers, the U.S. Mint's Web site, Michael White at the Mint's Office of Public Affairs and Judy Dixon's weekly sales report download. Rankings do not afford the luxury of population ranges preferred by classic coin scholars so a middle of the road number was selected and posted after looking at all the data. The ranking does, however, give us a ***general*** feel for the design-based rarity possessed by moderns.

Mint State Type Coin Ranking For the Last 200 Years

Rank	Population	Description	Price
1	100	1839 Liberty Seated Half -No Drapery	$27,000
2	100	1821-1827 Capped $2.5 Gold Large	$45,000
3	250	1829- 1834 Capped $2.5 Gold Small	$27,000
4	300	1829-1834 Capped Head $5 Gold Small	$72,000
5	400	1907 Indian $10 Gold with Periods & no Motto	$40,000
6	483	1915-S Panama-Pacific $50 Gold Round	$80,000
7	645	1915-S Panama-Pacific $50 Gold-Octagonal	$75,000
8	650	1808-1814 Classic Head Cent	$9,000
9	850	1838-1840 Liberty Seated Quarter No Drapery	$4,000
10	900	1837-1838 Liberty Seated Dime No Stars	$2,000
11	1,500	1838-1839 Capped Bust Half	$2,000
12	1,900	1854-1855 Liberty Seated Half Arrows	$1,450
13	2,000	1838-1840 Liberty Seated Dime No Drapery w. Stars	$700
14	2,000	1836-1837 Capped Bust Half Reeded Edge	$2,500
15	2,100	1853 Liberty Seated Half Arrows & Rays	$3,000
16	2,200	1838-1866 Liberty Head $10 Gold	$15,000
17	2,200	1813-1829 Capped Head $5 Gold Large	$20,000
18	2,253	2008-W $50 Mint State Platinum Eagle-Judicial	$1,200
19	2,300	1873-1874 Liberty Seated Half with Arrows	$2,000
20	2,481	2008-W $25 Mint State Platinum Eagle-Judicial	$600
21	2,500	1836-1839 Matron Head Cent	$400
22	2,500	1815-1828 Capped Bust Quarter-Large	$6,000
23	2,500	1854-1855 Liberty Seated Quarter Arrows	$1,100
24	2,500	1873-1874 Liberty Seated Quarter Arrows	$1,400
25	2,500	1807-1812 Capped Bust $5 Gold	$15,000
26	2,500	1834-1838 Classic Head $5 Gold	$6,000
27	2,577	2006-W $50 Mint State Platinum Eagle-Legislative	$1,200
28	2,676	2006-W $25 Mint State Platinum Eagle-Legislative	$500
29	2,750	1837-1838 Liberty Seated Half Dime	$1,000
30	2,750	1873-1874 Liberty Seated Dime Arrows	$1,200
31	2,876	2008-W $100 Mint State Platinum Eagle-Judicial	$1,900
32	3,000	1834-1839 Classic Head $2.5 Gold	$6,000
33	3,068	2006-W $100 Mint State Platinum Eagle-Legislative	$1,900

Mint State Type Coin Ranking For the Last 200 Years *continued*

Rank	Population	Description	Price
34	3,250	1838-1840 Liberty Seated Half Dime with Stars	$450
35	3,500	1853 Liberty Seated Quarter Arrows & Rays	$3,000
36	3,500	1866-1873 Liberty Seated Dollar With Motto	$4,500
37	3,544	2006-W $10 Mint State Platinum Eagle-Legislative	$400
38	3,635	2007-W $50 Mint State Platinum Eagle-Executive	$900
39	3,690	2007-W $25 Mint State Platinum Eagle-Executive	$450
40	3,706	2008-W $10 Mint State Platinum Eagle-Judicial	$200
41	4,000	1854-1858 Three Cent Silver 3 Outlines	$700
42	4,000	1809-1828 Capped Bust Dime Open Collar	$2,200
43	4,000	1853-1855 Liberty Seated Dime, Arrows	$600
44	4,177	2007-W $100 Mint State Platinum Eagle-Executive	$1,200
45	4,200	2008 Adams First Spouse $10 Gold	$600
46	4,300	2008 Van Buren's Liberty $10 Gold	$800
47	4,500	1907 High Relief Saint $20 Gold	$26,000
48	4,500	2008 Monroe First Spouse Gold	$600
49	4,700	2008 Jackson's Liberty $10 Gold	$750
50	5,000	1853-1855 Liberty Seated Half Dime -Arrows	$300
51	5,174	1997 Jackie Robinson $5 Gold	$4,000
52	5,250	1831-1838 Capped Bust Quarter-Small	$4,000
53	5,556	2007-W $10 Mint State Platinum Eagle-Executive	$180
54	6,000	1840-1860 Liberty Seated Dime, Drapery & Stars	$500
55	6,000	1828-1837 Capped Bust Dime Closed Collar	$1,600
56	6,500	1809-1836 Classic Head Half Cent	$500
57	6,500	1839-1866 Liberty Head $5 Gold	$8,000
58	6,683	2000 Library Of Congress Bimetallic $10	$4,000
59	6,749	1915s Panama-Pacific $2.5 Gold	$3,600
60	6,761	2001 Capital Visitor Center $5 Gold	$1,300
61	7,500	1840-1857 Braided Hair Half Cent	$500
62	7,500	1859 Indian Cent Laurel	$600
63	7,500	1875-1878 Twenty Cent Piece	$1,100
64	7,500	1854-1856 Indian Princess Gold Dollar Small Head	$17,000
65	8,000	1850-1866 Liberty Head $20 Gold Type I	$6,000
66	9,068	1996 Smithsonian $5 Gold	$850

Mint State Type Coin Ranking For the Last 200 Years *continued*

Rank	Population	Description	Price
67	9,174	1996 Flag Bearer $5 Gold	$2,000
68	9,210	1996 Cauldron $5 Gold	$2,000
69	9,949	2008-W $10 Mint State Buffalo Gold	$900
70	9,958	1928 Hawaiian Half	$3,000
71	10,000	1866-1867 Shield Nickel Rays	$400
72	10,008	1935 Hudson Half	$900
73	10,008	1935 Old Spanish Trail Half	$1,400
74	10,016	1922 Grant Gold Dollar	$2,000
75	10,129	2003 First Flight $10 Gold	$600
76	10,579	1995 Stadium $5 Gold	$2,000
77	10,585	2002 Salt Lake City $5 Gold	$400
78	11,000	1866-1876 Liberty Head $20 Gold Type II	$11,000
79	11,894	1997 Roosevelt $5 Gold	$1,500
80	12,000	1840-1859 Liberty Seated Half Dime, Drapery & Stars	$500
81	12,500	2007 Dolly Madison $10 Gold	$550
82	12,500	1816-1836 Matron Head Cent	$400
83	12,500	1856-1858 Flying Eagle Cent	$1,000
84	12,500	1859-1873 Three Cent Silver 2 Outlines	$400
85	12,500	1840-1865 Liberty Seated Quarter Drapery no Motto	$800
86	12,500	1840-1865 Liberty Seated Dollar no Motto	$3,800
87	12,735	1995 Civil War $5 Gold	$900
88	13,467	2008 Bald Eagle $5 Gold	$350
89	14,000	1860-1873 Liberty Seated Half Dime-Legend	$280
90	14,497	1996 Wheelchair Dollar	$320
91	14,675	1995 Torch Runner $5 Gold	$850
92	14,994	1925 Fort Vancouver Half	$400
93	15,000	1829-1837 Capped Bust Half Dime	$700
94	15,000	1839-1866 Liberty Seated Half Drapery, No Motto	$1,000
95	15,000	1915-S Panama-Pacific $1 Gold	$700
96	15,016	1936 Cincinnati Music Center Half	$350
97	15,266	1938 New Rochelle Half	$340
98	15,697	1996 High Jump Dollar	$330
99	15,983	1996 Tennis Dollar	$270

Mint State Type Coin Ranking For the Last 200 Years *continued*

Rank	Population	Description	Price
100	16,230	2006 San Francisco Mint $5 Gold	$350
101	16,258	1996 Rowing Dollar	$300
102	16,908	2008-W $25 Mint State Buffalo Gold	$1,200
103	16,936	1936 Norfolk Half	$400
104	17,429	2008-W $5 Mint State Buffalo Gold	$475
105	17,500	1903 Louisiana Purchase Jefferson $1 gold	$900
106	17,500	1903 Louisiana Purchase McKinley $1 Gold	$800
107	17,671	1936 Albany Half	$300
108	18,000	1866-1891 Liberty Seated Quarter with Motto	$425
109	18,028	1937 Antietam Half	$700
110	18,843	2007 Jamestown $5 Gold	$350
111	19,662	1995 Cycling Dollar	$125
112	20,000	1865-1889 Three Cent Nickel	$190
113	20,000	1866-1891 Liberty Seated Half with Motto	$1,000
114	20,000	1873-1885 Trade Dollar	$1,800
115	20,000	1916-17 McKinley $1 Gold	$600
116	20,000	2007 Martha Washington $10 Gold	$550
117	20,000	2007 Abigail Adams $10 Gold	$550
118	20,000	2007 Jefferson -Liberty Obverse $10 Gold	$550
119	20,013	1936 Lynchburg Virginia Half	$235
120	20,015	1936 Elgin Illinois Half	$215
121	20,066	1904-05 Lewis & Clark $1 Gold	$1,500
122	20,428	1921 Missouri Half	$800
123	20,993	1936 Delaware Half	$250
124	22,464	1994 World Cup $5 Gold	$350
125	22,511	1999 Washington $5 Gold	$400
126	23,089	1993 WWII $5 Gold	$425
127	23,266	1993 James Madison $5 Gold	$400
128	23,468	1996 Community Service Dollar	$180
129	23,614	1999 Yellowstone Dollar	$45
130	24,214	1893 Isabella Quarter	$700
131	24,329	1992 Columbus $5 Gold	$375
132	24,976	1995 Track and Field Dollar	$70

Mint State Type Coin Ranking For the Last 200 Years *continued*

Rank	Population	Description	Price
133	25,000	1860-1864 Indian Cent CN	$165
134	25,000	1851-1853 Three Cent Silver N.O.	$230
135	25,015	1934 Maryland Half	$165
136	25,015	1936 Wisconsin Half	$220
137	25,015	1936 York County Maine Half	$190
138	25,015	1936 Bridgeport Half	$160
139	25,018	1935 Connecticut Half	$250
140	25,023	1936 Columbia Half	$235
141	25,265	1936 Arkansas Robinson Half	$100
142	26,928	1936 Gettysburg Half	$440
143	27,134	1915s Panama-Pacific Half	$710
144	27,500	1864-1873 Two Cent Piece	$150
145	27,732	1992 Olympics $5 Gold	$375
146	28,142	1927 Vermont Half	$250
147	28,150	2000 Leif Ericson Dollar	$75
148	28,575	1997 Law Enforcement Dollar	$140
149	28,649	1995 Paralympics Dollar	$70
150	29,030	1936 Roanoke Half	$200
151	30,000	1839-1857 Braided Hair Cent	$170
152	30,000	1921 Peace Dollar High Relief	$400
153	30,000	1854-1889 Indian Head $3 Gold	$5,500
154	30,000	1907 Indian $10 Gold no Periods & no Motto	$3,200
155	30,007	1997 Jackie Robinson Dollar	$82
156	31,230	1996 Smithsonian Dollar	$110
157	31,959	1991 Mount Rushmore $5 Gold	$375
158	32,000	1892-1915 Barber Half	$650
159	32,000	1856-1889 Indian Princess Gold Dollars Large Head	$900
160	35,400	2001 Visitor Center Dollar	$28
161	36,026	1900 Lafayette Dollar	$1,750
162	37,210	1998 Black Patriots Dollar	$130
163	37,500	1849-1854 Liberty Head Gold Dollar	$900
164	40,257	2002 Salt Lake City Dollar	$27
165	42,497	1995 Gymnastics Dollar	$60

Rank	Population	Description	Price
166	42,500	1860-1891 Liberty Seated Dime Legend	$290
167	45,866	1995 Civil War Dollar	$62
168	46,019	1926 American Independence $2.5 Gold	$700
169	46,899	1989 Congress $5 Gold	$350
170	48,000	1916-1917 Standing Liberty Quarter Type I	$300
171	48,953	2005 John Marshall Silver Dollar	$28
172	49,533	1996 Swimming Half	$130
173	49,671	2005 Marine Corps Dollar	$34
174	50,028	1920 Maine Half	$165
175	50,030	1936 Cleveland Half	$100
176	50,034	1936 Providence Rhode Island Half	$100
177	52,771	2000 Library Of Congress Dollar	$35
178	52,836	1996 Soccer Half	$125
179	53,054	1994 Women in Military Service Dollar	$33
180	53,761	2003 First Flight Dollar	$30
181	54,790	1994 POW Dollar	$70
182	57,272	1997 Botanic Garden Dollar	$35
183	57,317	1994 Vietnam Dollar	$70
184	57,726	2003 First Flight Half	$12
185	61,956	2006 Benjamin Franklin Dollar-Scientist	$24
186	62,000	1807-1836 Capped Bust Half-Lettered Edge	$1,800
187	62,913	1988 Olympics $5 Gold	$325
188	64,014	2006 Benjamin Franklin Dollar-Founding Father	$25
189	65,044	1921 Alabama Half	$385
190	65,609	2006 San Francisco Dollar	$35
191	66,093	2007 Central High Dollar	$30
192	68,051	2004 Thomas Edison Dollar	$25
193	68,352	1994 Capital Dollar	$20
194	71,424	1936 Oakland Bay Bridge Half	$140
195	71,661	1922 Grant Half	$135
196	75,000	1992-1916 Barber Quarter	$280
197	75,886	1984 Los Angeles $10 Gold	$555
198	79,801	2007 Jamestown Dollar	$26

Mint State Type Coin Ranking For the Last 200 Years *continued*

Rank	Population	Description	Price
199	81,698	1994 World Cup Dollar	$20
200	81,826	1936 Long Island Half	$85
201	83,000	2009 Braille Dollar	$35
202	85,301	1935-1939 Arkansas Half	$100
203	85,000	1892-1916 Barber Dime	$130
204	86,394	1925 California Diamond Half	$255
205	87,187	1934-38 Boone Half	$115
206	88,000	1867-1883 Shield Nickel No Rays	$175
207	89,104	1999 Dolly Madison Dollar	$37
208	89,301	1995 Special Olympics Dollar	$26
209	90,323	2004 Lewis and Clark Dollar	$21
210	94,708	1993 WWII Dollar	$26
211	95,248	1986 Statue of Liberty $5 Gold	$325
212	98,383	1993 Bill of Rights Dollar	$20
213	99,157	2001 Capital Visitor Center Half	$12
214	100,057	1946 Iowa Half	$100
215	100,058	1918 Illinois Half	$150
216	100,224	1935-S-1936-D San Diego California Pacific Half	$100
217	103,201	2002 West Point Dollar	$20
218	106,422	1998 Robert Kennedy Dollar	$33
219	106,949	1992 Columbus Dollar	$23
220	110,073	2008 Bald Eagle Dollar	$28
221	119,520	1995 Civil War Half	$35
222	120,000	2008 Bald Eagle Half	$12
223	123,803	1992 White House Dollar	$22
224	124,958	1991 USO Dollar	$20
225	125,000	2009 Lincoln Dollar	$55
226	133,139	1991 Mount Rushmore Dollar	$25
227	135,203	1989 Congress Dollar	$20
228	135,702	1992 Christopher Columbus Half	$10
229	140,000	1908-1929 Indian $2.5 Gold	$900
230	141,120	1926 American Independence Half	$100
231	142,080	1924 Huguenot-Walloon Half	$125

Rank	Population	Description	Price
232	149,661	1934-1938 Texas Independence Half	$130
233	150,000	1864-1909 Indian Cent Bronze	$45
234	150,000	1849-1907 Liberty Head $2.5 Gold	$1,000
235	161,607	1992 XXV Olympiad Half	$8
236	162,013	1925 Lexington-Concord Half	$100
237	163,753	1989 Congress Half	$7
238	164,605	1995 Baseball Half	$18
239	168,204	1994 World Cup Half	$8
240	171,001	1995 Basketball Half	$18
241	172,165	1920-1921 Pilgrim Half	$95
242	172,754	1991 Mount Rushmore half	$18
243	187,552	1992 XXV Olympiad Dollar	$20
244	190,000	1883 V Nickel No Cents	$40
245	191,368	1988 Olympiad Dollar	$18
246	193,346	1993 Bill of Rights Half	$16
247	197,072	1993 WWII Half	$22
248	200,000	1913 Buffalo Nickel Raised Mound	$60
249	200,000	1917-1930 Standing Liberty Quarter Type II	$200
250	203,101	1926-1939 Oregon Trail Half	$150
251	213,049	1991 Korean War Dollar	$18
252	214,225	1987 Constitution $5 Gold	$325
253	227,131	2001 American Buffalo Dollar	$140
254	241,669	1990 Eisenhower Dollar	$18
255	266,927	1993 Jefferson Silver Dollar	$18
256	274,077	1923 Monroe Doctrine Half	$125
257	300,000	1908-1929 Indian $5 Gold	$1,700
258	325,000	1908-1933 Indian $10 Gold	$2,000
259	325,000	1907-1908 Saint $20 No Motto	$2,000
260	500,000	1877-1907 Liberty Head $20 Gold Type III	$2,400

The mint state type listing clearly shows:

1. Moderns account for one-third of the 100 rarest design and denomination-based mint state type coins in the last 200 years!

2. In terms of design-based type rarity, moderns are dramatically less expensive than older issues of similar mint state populations.

3. The U.S. Mint basically **suspended the production of serious mint state type coins with sub 8,000 populations after 1915** and did not resume the issuance of such material until 1997.

4. Great type coins old or new tend to have very short production periods. Regardless of how small the annual mintages are, if the series runs uninterrupted for 20-plus years, the type rarity of the issue is normally ruined. The Mint's long-standing policy of almost zero design change, which effectively started around 1840, is very telling in the listings.

Proof coinage issued prior to 1859 was sporadic. Proof gold eagle production that can be traced from Mint records began on a consistent basis in 1859. Let's look at every design and denomination-based proof type coin that has been issued since then to the general public with a population of 75,000 or less. Classics are priced at the grading center-line (PF-64 in most cases). Classic population estimates are only for coins surviving in PF-60 or better.

1907 High Relief
Saint-Gaudens
$20 Gold

1854-1889
Indian Head
$3 Gold

Proof Type Coin Ranking Since 1859

Rank	Population	Description	Price
1	125	1850-1866 Liberty $20 Gold	$100,000
2	150	1839-1866 Liberty $5 Gold	$40,000
3	150	1866-1876 Liberty $20 Gold with Motto 20D	$90,000
4	200	1839-1866 Liberty $10 Gold	$55,000
5	400	1966-1867 Shield Nickel With Rays	$2,000
6	500	1908-1915 Saint $20 Gold	$34,000
7	550	1908-1915 Indian $10 Gold	$22,000
8	600	1859 Indian Cent Laurel Wreath	$1,100
9	650	1913 Buffalo Nickel-Raised Mound Matte	$1,300
10	700	1908-1915 Indian $5 Gold	$19,000
11	1,000	1873-1874 Seated Half Arrows	$4,200
12	1,100	1873-1874 Seated Dime Arrows	$2,000
13	1,100	1873-1874 Seated Quarter Arrows	$3,400
14	1,300	1840-1859 Seated Half Dime, Drapery & 13 Stars	$2,000
15	1,300	1840-1860 Seated Dime, Drapery & Stars	$2,000
16	1,400	1908-1915 Indian $2.5 Gold	$12,000
17	1,600	1854-1889 Indian $3 Gold	$17,000
18	1,700	1866-1908 Liberty $10 Gold with Motto	$22,000
19	1,750	1860-1864 Indian Cent Oak Wreath Cop-Nickel	$1,000
20	1,800	1877-1907 Liberty $20 Gold with Motto	$45,000
21	2,200	1866-1908 Liberty $5 Gold with Motto	$17,500
22	3,000	1913-1915 Buffalo Nickel Flat Ground Matte	$950
23	3,000	1840-1907 Liberty $2.5 Gold	$11,000
24	4,000	1883 V Nickel no Cents	$350
25	4,000	1875-1878 Twenty Cent Piece	$4,300
26	4,000	2008 $50 Proof Platinum Eagle-Judicial	$1,400
27	4,000	1840-1865 Seated Quarter, Drapery, no Motto	$2,500
28	4,000	1939-1866 Seated Half Drapery, no Motto	$3,000
29	4,000	1840-1865 Seated Dollar no Motto	$6,500
30	4,200	2008 $25 Proof Platinum Eagle-Judicial	$700
31	4,600	1866-1873 Seated Dollar with Motto	$6,200
32	4,800	2008 $100 Platinum Eagle-Judicial	$2,200
33	5,063	2004 $50 Platinum Eagle-Seated America	$1,600

Proof Type Coin Ranking Since 1859 *continued*

Rank	Population	Description	Price
34	5,100	2008 $10 Platinum Eagle-Judicial	$400
35	5,193	2004 $25 Platinum Eagle-Seated America	$1,100
36	5,824	2007 $25 Platinum Eagle-Executive	$500
37	5,942	2005 $50 Platinum Eagle-Plenty	$950
38	6,007	2004 $100 Platinum Eagle-Seated America	$2,400
39	6,300	1856-1889 Indian Gold Dollar	$6,300
40	6,592	2005 $25 Platinum Eagle-Plenty	$500
41	6,602	2005 $100 Platinum Eagle-Plenty	$1,800
42	7,000	1859-1873 Three Cent Silver	$700
43	7,044	2003 $25 Platinum Eagle-Patriotic Vigilance	$425
44	7,131	2003 $50 Platinum Eagle-Patriotic Vigilance	$850
45	7,161	2004 $10 Platinum Eagle-Seated America	$600
46	7,400	2008 Adams First Spouse Gold	$600
47	7,500	1964-1873 Two Cent Piece	$550
48	7,500	2008 Van Buren First Spouse Gold	$700
49	7,649	2006 $50 Platinum Eagle-Legislative	$825
50	7,800	2006 $25 Platinum Eagle-Legislative	$400
51	7,800	2008 Jackson First Spouse	$700
52	7,900	2008 Monroe First Spouse Gold	$650
53	8,000	1860-1873 Seated Half Dime Legend	$700
54	8,000	1873-1885 Trade Dollar	$5,000
55	8,000	2009 $100 Platinum Eagle- Perfect Union	$1,700
56	8,006	2007 $10 Platinum Eagle-Executive	$200
57	8,104	2005 $10 Platinum Eagle-Plenty	$225
58	8,246	2003 $100 Platinum Eagle-Patriotic Vigilance	$1,800
59	8,254	2001 $50 Platinum Eagle-South West	$800
60	8,772	2002 $50 Platinum Eagle-North West	$800
61	8,847	2001 $25 Platinum Eagle-South West	$400
62	8,969	2001$100 Platinum Eagle-South West	$1,800
63	9,000	1909-1915 Lincoln Cent Matte Wheat	$700
64	9,000	1936-1937 Buffalo Nickel Mirror	$1,300
65	9,152	2006 $100 Platinum Eagle-Legislative	$1,800
66	9,268	2007 $100 Platinum Eagle-Executive	$1,600

Proof Type Coin Ranking Since 1859 *continued*

Rank	Population	Description	Price
67	9,282	2002 $25 Platinum Eagle-North West	$400
68	9,534	2003 $10 Platinum Eagle-Patriotic Vigilance	$235
69	9,834	2002 $100 Platinum Eagle-North West	$1,600
70	9,996	2006 $50 20th Anniv. Gold Eagle	2,800
71	10,205	2006 $10 Platinum Eagle-Legislative	$175
72	11,049	2000 $50 Platinum Eagle-Heart Land	$800
73	11,103	1999 $50 Platinum Eagle-Wet Lands	$800
74	11,995	2000 $25 Platinum Eagle-Heart Land	$400
75	12,000	1892-1916 Barber Quarter	$1,200
76	12,169	2008 $25 Buffalo Gold	$1,600
77	12,174	2001$10 Platinum Eagle-South West	$170
78	12,363	1999 $100 Platinum Eagle-Wet Lands	$1,600
79	12,365	2002 $10 Platinum Eagle-North West	$160
80	12,453	2000 $100 Platinum Eagle-Heart Land	$1,600
81	13,000	1892-1916 Barber Dime	$800
82	13,000	1891-1915 Barber Half	$1,600
83	13,125	2008 $10 Buffalo Gold	$900
84	13,507	1999 $25 Platinum Eagle-Wet Lands	$400
85	13,836	1998 $50 Platinum Eagle-New England	$800
86	14,873	1998 $25 Platinum Eagle-New England	$400
87	14,912	1998 $100 Platinum Eagle-New England	$1,600
88	15,431	1997 $50 Platinum Eagle-Eagle Over Sun	$800
89	15,651	2000 $10 Platinum Eagle-Heart Land	$150
90	16,000	1878-1904 Morgan Dollar	$3,800
91	16,937	2007 $50 Platinum Eagle-Presidential Rev. Proof	$1,000
92	17,000	1866-1891 Seated Half with Motto	$1,800
93	18,000	1866-1891 Seated Quarter with Motto	$1,300
94	18,300	2007 Madison $10 First Spouse Gold	$550
95	18,628	1997 $25 Platinum Eagle-Eagle Over Sun	$400
96	18,884	2008 $5 Buffalo Gold	$400
97	19,133	1999 $10 Platinum Eagle-Wet Lands	$150
98	19,847	1998 $10 Platinum Eagle-New England	$150
99	20,000	1860-1891Seated Dime Legend	$850

Proof Type Coin Ranking Since 1859 *continued*

Rank	Population	Description	Price
100	20,000	2007 Washington First Spouse $10 Gold	$550
101	20,000	2007 Adams First Spouse $10 Gold	$550
102	20,000	2007 Jefferson's Liberty $10 Gold	$550
103	20,851	1997 $100 Platinum Eagle- Eagle Over Sun	$1,700
104	21,840	1996 Smithsonian $5 Gold	$500
105	21,846	2003 First Flight $10 Gold	$550
106	22,873	2007 $50 Platinum Eagle-Executive	$800
107	24,072	1997 Jackie Robinson $5 Gold	$525
108	25,000	1867-1883 Shield Nickel no Rays	$400
109	27,167	2000 Library of Congress $10 Bimetallic	$975
110	27,600	1942 Jefferson Silver Nickel	$100
111	27,652	2001 Capital Visitor Center $5 Gold	$380
112	29,233	1997 Roosevelt $5 Gold	$325
113	32,877	2002 Salt Lake $5 Gold	$325
114	32,886	1996 Flag Bearer $5 Gold	$565
115	36,993	1997 $10 Platinum Eagle-Eagle Over Sun	$150
116	38,555	1996 Cauldron $5 Gold	$525
117	40,000	1865-1889 Three Cent Nickel	$400
118	41,693	1999 George Washington $5 Gold	$330
119	43,124	1995 Stadium $5 Gold	$520
120	44,000	2006 San Francisco Mint $5 Gold	$325
121	47,050	2007 Jamestown $5 Gold	$325
122	55,246	1995 Civil War $5 Gold	$375
123	57,442	1995 Torch Runner $5 Gold	$335
124	59,000	2008 Bald Eagle $5 Gold	$325
125	60,000	1864-1909 Indian Cent Bronze	$250
126	60,000	1883-1913 V Nickel with Cents	$300
127	65,000	1936-1942 Walking Liberty Half	$700
128	70,000	1936-1942 Mercury Dime	$200

This proof type listing teaches us several important lessons:

1. Small denomination proof type coinage, especially those struck on copper and nickel, do not attract the same kind of wealthy collector base that the high denomination, high material content type coins do.

2. Proof coins that are type rare based on something other that a substantial change to the coin's physical appearance and whose similar appearing siblings have large total populations do not command anything like the price they should based solely on the shown populations of the subset. An obvious example of this is the Seated fractional silver with arrows beside the date issued from 1873-1874. The coins are basically identical to the succeding years out to 1891 and it takes the edge off their values.

3. Notice that out of the 70+ plus proof coins in production since 1859 with sub 10,000 surviving high grade populations, 29 of them are the changing reverse cameo proof platinum eagles.

4. The modern proofs are in their infancy and are extremely inexpensive based on their design and denomination based type rarity.

1873-1885
Trade Dollar

1878-1904
Morgan Dollar

1836 Gobrecht Dollar

CHAPTER 7

MODERNS AND CLASSICS:
IN THE SAME FAMILY?

There are some classic collectors who believe that modern U.S. Mint issues are type rare and although some have astonishingly low mintages, they do not qualify as "coins" because they are not issued to the public at face value and used in common commerce. In their view, being issued under the authority of Congress and struck by the U.S. Mint as legal tender is just a gimmick to sell bullion to the public at a premium.

Benjamin Franklin once said that *"the murder of a beautiful theory by a gang of brutal facts" is a terrible thing, and we can clearly demonstrate that here.* The last 200 years and the market's pricing structure speak clearly on the issue. Let's look at a few examples.

1. From 1821 to 1834, half eagles and quarter eagles had higher bullion value than face value. They did not circulate but they could be bought at a premium from bullion dealers. The melting and shipment of the bullion overseas was so pervasive that coins like the 1822 half eagle with an initial mintage of 17,796 coins has only three known survivors.

2. Many surviving high grade Gobrecht dollars (flying eagle reverse) were struck by the Mint for collectors from 1850 to 1870 and sold for a premium over face. High grade Gobrecht dollars in any form are worth $20,000-$50,000 each today. Most high-grade survivors were not even legal tender at the time of issue.

3. Proof Draped Bust dollars known as "restrikes" dated from 1801 through 1804 were struck in the late 1800s. They were sold or traded at a premium, were not intended for circulation and Congress did not sanction their production. Almost any attractive example is over $50,000 now.

4. Trade dollars that went into production in 1873 were intended as bullion coins for export. The early issues contained higher bullion value than face value. By 1876, Trade dollars could be purchased for 91 cents and Congress terminated the Trade dollar's status as legal tender. Nonetheless, the U.S. Mint at Philadelphia continued to issue the coins as proofs for a premium well into the mid-1880s. These non-legal tender coins are valued at over $2,000 each for nice examples.

5. 1915 Panama Pacific $50 commemoratives were struck on approximately 2 ounces of gold, were not intended for circulation and sold to the public for $100 each. That was the typical worker's wages for one month and the special issues were not well received. Today $50 Pan-Pac gold commems command between $35,000 and $125,000 each.

6. Almost all the classic silver commemorative halves issued between 1892 and 1945 were sold at a premium over face value, were legal tender and were not struck intended for circulation.

This listing could be extended but the point is clear. **The market long term does not care what the issue price was, how it related to intrinsic value or if the Mint intended for them to circulate or even exist. If the U.S. Mint struck the coins and put a dollar-based denomination on them the market has a long and clear history of embracing the issue.**

CHAPTER 8

PRECIOUS METALS PRICES AND NUMISMATIC PREMIUMS

Disposable Income, Material Content and Risk

The sky-high premiums over intrinsic value for rare classic coins that have developed over the years are directly correlated with disposable income growth of the populace and the net influx of collectors who subscribe to the series date and mintmark collecting structure. If anything were to happen to reduce real disposable income or change collecting habits it could produce dramatic losses or adversely affect the market's liquidity because the classic set's intrinsic value in mint state grades is frequently only 2 cents on the dollar or less.

Attractive series with massive total populations with relatively small mintage infant keys are what create opportunities for growth. Buying coins struck on the precious metals for a fraction over their cost to mine the material (like platinum at $1,000/oz) give you an almost bulletproof floor that you can count on and it's always very liquid. Blending the two is the perfect solution, if you can find it. But can we find it? There are at least a dozen modern sets that may prove to fit that profile. Let's look at three at random.

	Complete Set Price	Value First 4 Keys	Intrinsic Value
$10 Gold Eagles MS-69	$10,000	$2,800	$7,000
$25 Platinum Eagles PR-69	$6,000	$2,800	$4,000
$1 Commemoratives MS-69	$4,000	$1,200	$800

What most casual observers don't realize is there are going to be very few of these sets. The best data available indicates that less than 6,000 complete $10 gold eagles sets can be assembled, less than 4,200 $25 proof platinum eagle sets, and 14,500 silver dollar Commemorative sets. The keys have plenty of room for growth and high material content affords you a degree of protection if the collector markets suffer from some form of unforeseen hardship.

Common Dates Sold for Melt and its Effect On Keys

As clearly demonstrated previously, the common date sets being put together by collectors are what force a premium on the lowest mintage issues in any set. Key issue value growth is impressive as a result until material prices dramatically surpass the collector value of the common dates or disposable income drops. Let's see how high precious metal prices can cause key date premiums to evaporate.

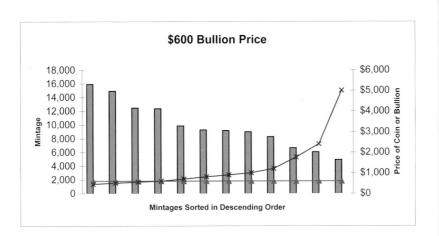

$600 Bullion Price

This is the same old relative rarity price curve with a horizontal gold line representing the value of the bullion the coins are struck on added to it. The blue line is the fair market value of each coin. In this case only the two most common issues would have a lower price if they were struck on less metal. For the purposes of this discussion we will call having less numismatic value than bullion value "under water" coins.

In reality, the two most common dates will trade at about $625 and all the others will track the blue relative rarity price line.

Complete set value for 12 one ounce coins= $15,850
Set bullion value = $7,200

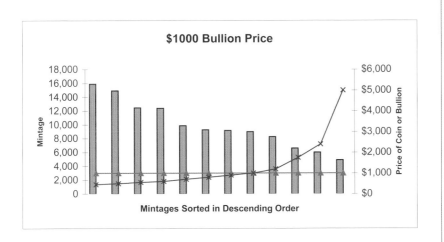

$1000 Bullion Price

In this case the material price has moved up to the point that half the members of the set are "under water." Collectors aren't excited about paying a little over $1,000 each for the first six common dates so they have the tendency to buy the sub 10,000 mintage issues first and work forward and backwards from there. The keys are unaffected so far.

Complete set value for 12 one ounce coins = $18,350
Set bullion value = $12,000

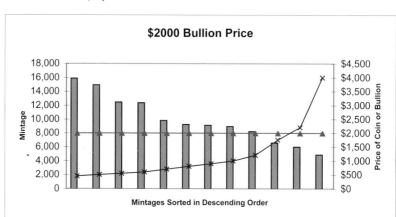

Material prices have spiked hard and collectors will not pay $2,000 each for what they perceive as common date material. Those who are not emotionally attached to their sets start selling. Sets start flooding into bullion houses like Kitco and SilverTowne because they are the highest bidders for the common dates. Only the two rarest are spared. With so many sets dissolved and individuals having nothing left but key dates, the price of the keys start to suffer.

The common dates are being sold into noncollector hands. Various forms of hardship may be their lot and many will not return to the collector market in the condition they left if at all. One of the so-called common coins could end up being the hardest to find in the out years. This is one way a "dark horse" can come in and supercede the coin the mintage tables indicate leads the set.

Complete set value for 12 one ounce coins = $26,200
Sets bullion value = $24,000

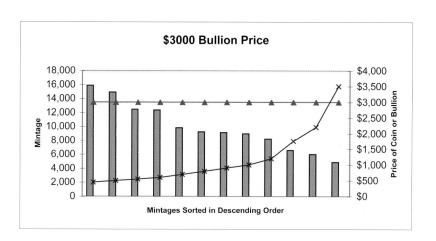

$3000 Bullion Price

Mintages Sorted in Descending Order

The material price spike has become SO severe that the highest bidder for almost all the members of the set are the bullion houses. Only the key is spared and it is traded for just a fraction over melt. The sets being sold are seeing hardship and the average condition of the coins is likely to deteriorate over time. The whole set in high grade is getting rarer all the time with the exception of the so called (at this point) key.

Complete set value for 12 one ounce coins = $36,500
Sets bullion value = $36,000

Notice in this scenario that collectors who just bought the key date and expected to see the typical high return associated with keys will be disappointed. The set collectors and the bullion buyers came out ahead. Small denomination coins with high material content are much more resistant to going "under water" and having their keys become semi-keys through this process.

Falling Disposable Income in the Midst of Governmental Money Creation

Now let's look at what happens when disposable income drops. The first chart shows a strong economy and mild material prices and the second chart assumes a recession has set in with the typical 30 percent price retrenchment on all coins other than those already trading at melt.

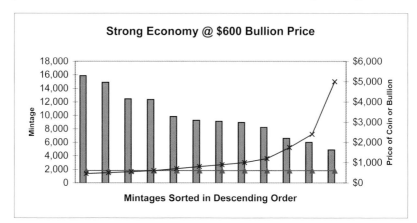

Complete set value for 12 one ounce coins = $15,850
Sets bullion value = $7,200

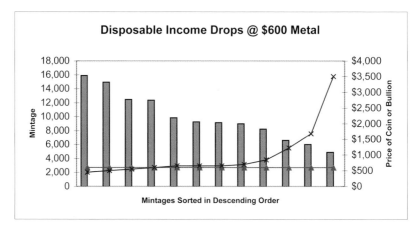

Initial Complete Set Value= $15,850
Sets Bullion Value = $7,200
Final Set Value During Recession= $12,300

The full set collector has lost about $3,500 and the bullion floor has blunted the collection's drop.

Below is the structure that is exhibiting itself in high material content collections in the serious recession that started in 2008 when the Federal Reserve tried to compensate with money supply growth.

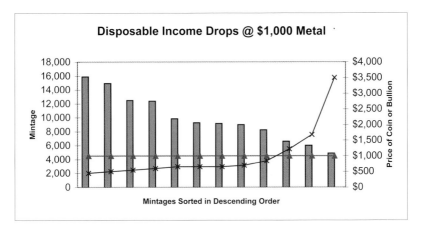

Disposable Income Drops @ $1,000 Metal

Mintages Sorted in Descending Order

Initial Complete Set Value= $15,850
Sets Bullion Value = $12,000
Final Set Value During Recession= $15,400

High bullion content complete sets retain their liquidity and value even if disposable income drops as long as the metals are up slightly from governmental money creation in serious a recession.

There are several messages here:

1. As long as times are good infant key dates are the best place put your hard earned collecting dollars.

2. If precious metals spike hard on high material content coins it can damage key date values, but if you collect the whole set you emerge in good shape anyway.

3. Series with mild precious metal content and high collector premiums are very vulnerable to drops in real disposable income or shifts in collector preference because they don't have a precious metal floor to catch them.

4. Fractional key date coins be they old or new are more resistant to material price spikes than their larger denomination siblings.

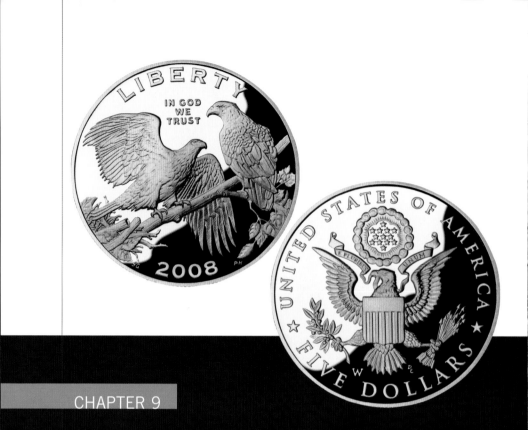

CHAPTER 9

COMMON PITFALLS: THINGS TO REMEMBER

Gradeflation, Crack Outs & Special Tags

Recently the major grading services have offered special attractive tags on their slabs with adages like "First Strike" and "Early Release." Some market participants pay exorbitant premiums over the basic coin's value because they are "low population tags."

There are many problems with this. If the prestige of the grading company in question is eclipsed by another grader at some point, the special label value can suffer. And, over time, we may see a proliferation of tags.

The crack out game is rampant for both classics and moderns. To illustrate the impact of this practice on the grading companies' population report, roughly 100 attractive "W" mintmarked moderns purchased directly from the U.S. Mint in single issue packaging were sent to NGC and PCGS grading services in small lots. The coins that did not make MS-70 were cracked out and sent back in up to four times. These are the percentages of the submissions and resubmissions that made grade each time. Many dealers are able to achieve grade through rates that are better than those shown.

Submission	NGC 70		PCGS 70	
1	71%	71 coins	28%	28 coins
2	41%	12 coins	32%	23 coins
3	29%	5 coins	22%	11 coins
4	18%	2 coins	18%	7 coins
5	10%	1 coin	16%	5 coins

Totals after five crack out cycles:
91 percent made NGC 70   74 percent made PCGS 70

The NGC population report in this case shows 91 coins made 70 out of 168 submissions yielding a 54 percent grade-through rate. The PCGS population report indicates that 74 coins made MS-70 out of 291 submitted giving us a 25 percent grade-through rate.

Be careful. Real rarity is the absence of attractive coins struck, sold and preserved, not the ever evolving tags and grading standards. High mintage moderns with custom tags graded "70 early/first/etc." with an "ultra low population" selling for multiples of the typical coins trading price are risky and should be avoided. *Coins that are perfect to the naked eye in 70s slabs bought at less than 1.5 times raw (69 grade) price can be good values. Be picky and "buy the coin not just the holder."*

Some dealers would point out that the grade-through rates of individually packaged moderns sold directly to the public is much higher than the grade-through rate of the series members that are issued in bulk through the dealer network . That's certainly true, but if the bulk issued coin has a dramatically higher mintage than the single issue coin then the bulk issue will also have to possess an extremely low 70 grade-though rate in order to warrant premiums much higher than 1.5 times the typical MS-69 price mentioned previously. A few exceptional coins

coins like the 1999-W $5, 1999-W $10 and 1991 $25 gold eagles are in fact low mintage and only a small percentage of them can grade MS-70 because of bulk handling practices. These coins and maybe a handful of moderns like them are rare in MS-70 form and justifiably command dramatically higher prices than their MS-69 siblings.

$10 Gold Eagle Reverse

Erosion of 70 Grade Premiums After Initial Issue

When a new issue first goes on sale at the Mint many of the larger dealers and flippers will buy the coins immediately and send them to PCGS or NGC for grading. The coins that graded MS-70 or PR-70 will then be put up for sale as soon as possible because dealers realize those who collect the series in question in NGC or PCGS 70 are a finite number at any given time.

With populations still near zero and almost all the MS/PR-70 collectors with holes in their sets, it's easy to unload the coins at relatively high margins in the first few weeks of sales. Some dealers will then buy a new batch from the Mint and return the lesser coins under the new Mint invoices or just send the already submitted coins back in to be graded again. The MS/PR-70 graded populations grow quickly and the number of MS/PR-70s collectors without the new issue in hand drops just as quickly. This process tends to repeat itself until a bottom is reached later in the production year while the raw coins are still on sale at the Mint. Most of the current collector base that wanted one has one and the dealers' leftover MS-70 inventory needs to be "turned" at whatever small markup the market will bear.

Classic High Grade Markets Indexed to Inflation

The chart on page 83 shows the behavior of several important market segments indexed to inflation and relative to constant dollar gold. The charts were developed based on goldprice.org's archives, backdated *Coin Dealer* newsletters, and CPI-U inflation tables.

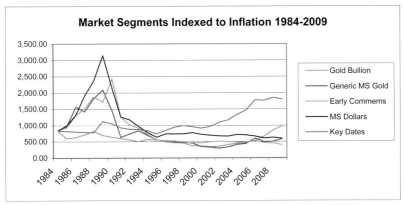

Market Segments Indexed to Inflation 1984-2009

Legend:
- Gold Bullion
- Generic MS Gold
- Early Commems
- MS Dollars
- Key Dates

Coinage indexed from the Coin Dealer newsletter archives, POB 7939, Torrance CA 90504, www.graysheet.com, Copyright CDN Inc 2010.

Common Coinage and Promotions

Starting around 1986, "investment firms" saw an opportunity to promote third-party graded mint state coinage to the public. They bought large quantities of relatively common mint state classic coinage in high grade and sold it to noncollectors at high mark ups. As a direct result of this aggressive marketing the price on these coins skyrocketed. Generic mint state gold prices more than doubled, silver commemorative halves tripled, and mint state Morgan and Peace dollar prices quadrupled in four years! The situation become unsustainable and prices crashed in dramatic fashion and have never recovered indexed to inflation. Post-1991 crash prices on mint state relatively common U.S. coinage in these market segments have not even been able to keep pace with inflation or gold bullion.

1895 Morgan Dollar

1922 Peace Dollar

High Bullion Content Classics

Classic generic MS60-65 gold has redeemed itself slightly over the last five years because its high material content is dictating to a large extent the price of the coinage. The collector premiums as a percentage of the total purchase price of this class of coin has been deteriorating in an uneven fashion for over 10 years. For modern or old coinage, don't pay multiples of melt for common "high grade" material regardless of how good the sales pitch or impressive the label is.

Key Dates: The Strong Red Line

Low population key date coinage wasn't aggressively marketed in the 1986 to 1990 investment mania largely because they could not "get enough of it to promote". Legitimate scarcity is a serious problem if you need to come up with enough material to fill two hundred $25,000 orders per month. *Key date material didn't spike much nor did it crash, it just continued its relentless march. Classic key dates have been pulling hard for a VERY long time* but we need to bear in mind that not even California's mighty Sequoia grows to the sky.

Coin Dealer Proverbs

Try to keep these insightful comments in mind when you are buying coins.

A farmer who sold baked vegetables at the county fair brought a barrel of still very hot vegetables back to the barn and dumped them all in the trough for the pigs. The hogs would come rushing over to get their share and get burned in the process.

His son asked, " There is more than enough for all of them, why don't they just wait until the food cools off so they don't get burned?"

The farmer said, "They are afraid they won't get any."

– Bill Kearce, GNS Eagles.

The Three Great Commandments of Coin Buying

1) "Buy the best."

2) "Risk not your whole wad at once."

3) "Buy the good stuff when it's cheap." People always want good material and if you buy it right you won't get hurt.

– Larry Pyle, Palmetto Galleries

"Real rarity is the absence of coins" not packaging.

– Hank Swain, 4th generation collector

If you buy coins that are high quality and rare before the herd arrives your odds are favorable. If a coin has had a big run recently or is a gold or platinum modern trading at over 10 times melt already you might want to find another issue or series to focus on. Remain flexible.

CHAPTER 10

THE SERIES

Lincoln Cent Type Set—
Winds of Change in the Longest U.S. Series

This great series is the longest running and most populous of all U.S. issues and as such has attracted a dedicated following. As of this writing there are at least eight mint state type coins that are profoundly different in physical appearance. They are listed at below:

Years Struck	Lincoln Cents by Type & Reverse	MS Mintage Totals
50	1909-1958 Wheat Reverse	over 10 billion
50	1959-2008 Lincoln Memorial Reverse	over 100 billion
1	1943 Steel War Issue	over 1 billion
1	2009 Childhood Reverse	635 million
1	2009 Formative Years	740 million
1	2009 Professional Life	652 million
1	2009 Presidency Reverse	327 million
?	2010 Preservation Reverse	

Will future generations of collectors tend to undertake a series with over 250 members, not counting die varieties, or just acquire a type set? We don't know because the type set likely doesn't have enough size to dominate the Lincoln cent set structure like we see in other series. If you think the proof Lincoln cents have a chance of becoming collected by type then 1909-1915 matte proof Lincolns with their roughly 9,000 total population are strong proof keys and the life of Lincoln proofs are noteworthy semi keys.

The very existence of the denomination in the U.S. Mint's production schedule is in doubt long term. The consistent march of inflation has ruined the usefulness of the cent and created a situation where the Mint can't recover their total cost when they strike it. The U.S. suspended the half cent is 1857 when it had a present value of 11 cents because its worth was deemed too small for daily commerce so a revision to the cent is long over due. Lincoln is justifiably well loved by the public and Congress so his image may endure on our coinage but what will be the denomination and coinage metal? It will be interesting to see how these changes will influence the development of the venerable Lincoln cent.

Jefferson Nickel Type Set—
The Last Remnant of Sound Money

The venerable nickel is the only current U.S. Mint issue for circulation that has its original material content dating all the way back to the 1866 Shield nickel. It is the last remnant of sound money in the U.S. When nickel prices spiked in 2006 through early 2008 the Mint's total cost per unit was almost 10 cents. Material costs have dropped back, but the Mint is still writing the public a check with every roll they issue at face value. It's amazing because the Federal government didn't let the price of silver coinage get anywhere close to twice melt before eliminating silver in 1964. It's not a question of if, but when will the Jefferson "nickel" fade from circulation in its current specifications?

1866 Shield Nickel

1938-2003

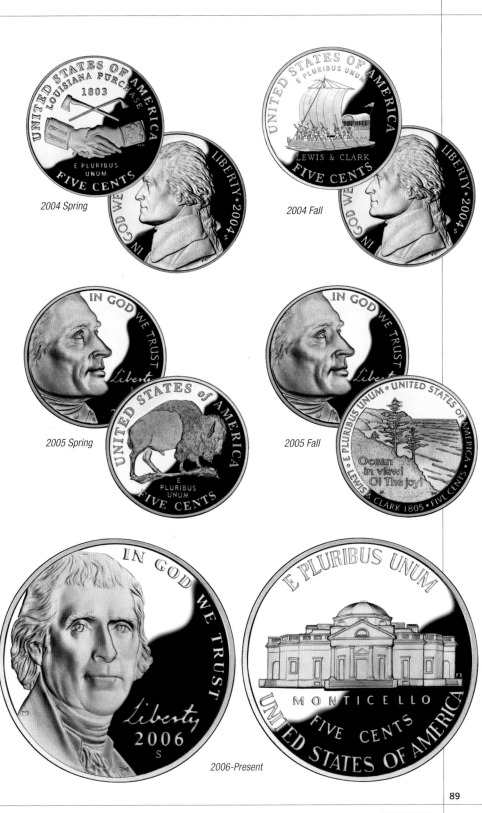

2004 Spring

2004 Fall

2005 Spring

2005 Fall

2006-Present

Business Strikes – Seven Major Types	Total Type Mintage	Mint State Price
Original Design Monticello	40 Billion +	$0.25
1942-1945 "Silver" Alloy Issues	869 Million	$5.00
2004 Peace Metal Issue	733 Million	$0.50
2004 Keelboat Issue	710 Million	$0.25
2005 Bison Issue	936 Million	$0.25
2005 Ocean In View	805 Million	$0.25
2006-Present Return to Monticello	Billions	$0.05

The mint state Jefferson nickels are an almost endless set, much like the Lincoln cents. Those who take an interest in this series but just want to go with a type set may find that outstanding silver nickels are the toughest coin in the set. The problem is too many war nickels were saved, and it is going to be hard to generate serious collector base compression even if collecting mint state Jeffersons by type becomes the rage.

Proofs – Seven Major Types	Total Type Mintage	Proof 65 Price
Original Design Monticello	75 million +	$3
1942 WW II "Silver" Alloy Issue	27,000	$100
2004 Peace Metal Issue	3 million	$6
2004 Keelboat Issue	3 million	$6
2005 Bison Issue	3.3 million	$3
2005 Ocean In View	3.3 million	$3
2006-Present Return to Monticello	10 million +	$3

If you think that collecting proof Jefferson nickels by type has any chance of becoming a dominant collecting form in this series then this simple listing speaks volumes. The proof World War II "silver" nickel is over 100 times rarer than its next closest sibling, and the set has a total population of about 100 million coins. That's an astoundingly tight bottleneck by any measure. Just as we saw in the 150-year proof type ranking it's the single year issues that tend to possess the most type strength all else equal and that's certainly the case with the 1942 proof silver nickel.

Fifty States & Territories Quarter Type Set

MODERN COMMEMORATIVE COINS

50 States/Territory Business Strike/Mint State	Mintage	MS-63
1999-P Delaware	373,400,000	$0.75
1999-D Delaware	401,424,000	$0.75
1999-P Pennsylvania	349,000,000	$0.75
1999-D Pennsylvania	358,332,000	$0.75
1999-P New Jersey	363,200,000	$0.70
1999-D New Jersey	299,028,000	$0.70
1999-P Georgia	451,188,000	$1.50
1999-D Georgia	488,744,000	$1.50
1999-P Connecticut	688,744,000	$1.00
1999-D Connecticut	657,880,000	$1.00
2000-P Massachusetts	629,800,000	$0.50
2000-D Massachusetts	535,184,000	$0.50
2000-P Maryland	678,200,000	$0.90
2000-D Maryland	556,500,000	$0.90
2000-P South Carolina	742,700,000	$1.00
2000-D South Carolina	566,208,000	$1.00
2000-P New Hampshire	673,040,000	$0.50
2000-D New Hampshire	495,976,000	$0.50
2000-P Virginia	943,000,000	$0.50
2000-D Virginia	651,616,000	$0.50
2001-P New York	655,400,000	$0.50
2001-D New York	619,940,000	$0.50
2001-P North Carolina	627,600,000	$0.50
2001-D North Carolina	427,876,000	$0.50
2001-P Rhode Island	423,000,000	$0.50
2001-D Rhode Island	447,100,000	$0.50
2001-P Vermont	423,400,000	$0.60
2001-D Vermont	459,404,000	$0.60
2001-P Kentucky	353,000,000	$0.50
2001-D Kentucky	370,564,000	$0.50
2002-P Tennessee	361,600,000	$1.25
2002-D Tennessee	286,468,000	$1.25
2002-P Ohio	217,200,000	$0.50
2002-D Ohio	414,832,000	$0.50
2002-P Louisiana	362,000,000	$0.50
2002-D Louisiana	402,204,000	$0.50
2002-P Indiana	362,600,000	$0.50
2002-D Indiana	327,200,000	$0.50
2002-P Mississippi	290,000,000	$0.50

50 States/Territory Business Strike/Mint State	Mintage	MS-63
2002-D Mississippi	289,600,000	$0.50
2003-P Illinois	225,800,000	$1.00
2003-D Illinois	237,400,000	$1.00
2003-P Alabama	225,000,000	$0.60
2003-D Alabama	232,400,000	$0.60
2003-P Maine	217,400,000	$0.50
2003-D Maine	231,400,000	$0.50
2003-P Missouri	225,000,000	$0.50
2003-D Missouri	228,200,000	$0.50
2003-P Arkansas	228,000,000	$0.50
2003-D Arkansas	229,800,000	$0.50
2004-P Michigan	233,800,000	$0.50
2004-D Michigan	225,800,000	$0.50
2004-P Florida	240,200,000	$0.50
2004-D Florida	241,600,000	$0.50
2004-P Texas	278,800,000	$0.50
2004-D Texas	263,000,000	$0.50
2004-P Iowa	213,800,000	$0.50
States/Ter.	Mintage	MS-63
2004-D Iowa	251,400,000	$0.50
2004-P Wisconsin	226,400,000	$0.50
2004-D Wisconsin	226,800,000	$0.50
Wisconsin-High	<50,000	$150
Wisconsin-Low	<50,000	$125
2005-P California	257,200,000	$0.50
2005-D California	263,200,000	$0.50
2005-P Minnesota	239,600,000	$0.50
2005-D Minnesota	248,400,000	$0.50
2005-P Oregon	316,200,000	$0.50
2005-D Oregon	404,000,000	$0.50
2005-P Kansas	263,400,000	$0.50
2005-D Kansas	300,000,000	$0.50
2005-P West Virginia	365,400,000	$0.50
2005-D West Virginia	356,200,000	$0.50
2006-P Nevada	277,000,000	$0.50
2006-D Nevada	312,800,000	$0.50
2006-P Nebraska	318,000,000	$0.50
2006-D Nebraska	276,400,000	$0.50
2006-P Colorado	274,800,000	$0.50

50 States/Territory Business Strike/Mint State	Mintage	MS-63
2006-D Colorado	294,200,000	$0.50
2006-P North Dakota	305,800,000	$0.50
2006-D North Dakota	359,000,000	$0.50
2006-P South Dakota	245,000,000	$0.50
2006-D South Dakota	265,800,000	$0.50
2007-P Idaho	294,600,000	$0.50
2007-D Idaho	286,800,000	$0.50
2007-P Montana	257,000,000	$0.50
2007-D Montana	256,240,000	$0.50
2007-P Utah	255,000,000	$0.50
2007-D Utah	253,200,000	$0.50
2007-P Washington	265,200,000	$0.50
2007-D Washington	280,000,000	$0.50
2007-P Wyoming	243,600,000	$0.50
2007-D Wyoming	320,800,000	$0.50
2008-P Oklahoma	222,000,000	$0.50
2008-D Oklahoma	194,600,000	$0.50
2008-P New Mexico	244,200,000	$0.50
2008-D New Mexico	244,400,000	$0.50
2008-P Arizona	244,600,000	$0.50
2008-D Arizona	265,000,000	$0.50
2008-P Alaska	251,800,000	$0.50
2008-D Alaska	254,000,000	$0.50
2008-P Hawaii	254,000,000	$0.50
2008-D Hawaii	263,600,000	$0.50
2009-P DC	83,600,000	$0.50
2009-D DC	88,800,000	$0.50
2009-P Puerto Rico	86,000,000	$0.50
2009-D Puerto Rico	53,200,000	$0.50
2009-P Guam	45,000,000	$0.50
2009-D Guam	42,600,000	$0.50
2009-P American Samoa	39,600,000	$0.50
2009-D American Samoa	42,600,000	$0.50
2009-P Virgin Islands	41,000,000	$0.50
2009-D Virgin Islands	41,000,000	$0.50
2009-P Mariana Islands	35,200,000	$0.50
2009-D Mariana Islands	37,600,000	$0.50

MODERN COMMEMORATIVE COINS

This set is the first circulating example of what the Mint calls a "collector series" with changing reverses. In a comparatively short period of time it has acquired what the Mint estimates to be 100 million adherents, a staggering number of collectors by any measure. Along with this unprecedented public interest has come an unprecedented number of rolls set aside for posterity, so as long as the economy preformed well, business strike mintages remained high and were absorbed by the public in large numbers. That changed in 2009 when people started depositing their extra coinage with their banks and ultimately back loaded the Treasury with far more coinage than they can store or process. This is a perfect example of a troubled infancy issue, and it is creating the lowest mintage business strike quarters since 1962.

This is the business strike 50 states and territories mintage profile. The 12 lowest mintages are the territories quarters. The mintage crash has been dramatic.

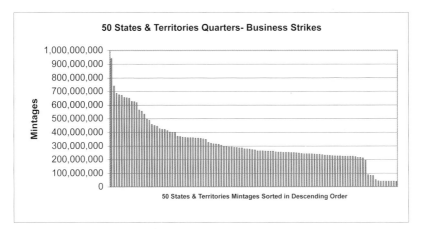

The following chart pulled from the section on how keys are created shows that three years of very low mintages could be at hand for circulating series.

There is little doubt that the Territory quarters will be the non-die variety keys to this set and if the coinage continues to backflow from the public to the Treasury we may find that the 2010 America the Beautiful quarters are the runaway keys to that set also.

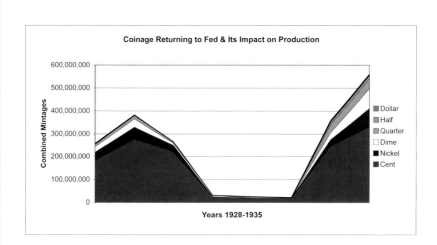

Coinage Returning to Fed & Its Impact on Production

Combined Mintages — Years 1928-1935

Legend: Dollar, Half, Quarter, Dime, Nickel, Cent

This situation is reminiscent of the 1950-D nickels. They too had extremely low mintages for business strike coinage and everybody knew it. There were very few struck but their retention rate by collectors was high. The rolls price spiked hard and then crashed in inflation adjusted numbers. Today a nice circulated 1950-D nickel brings almost as much as a mint state example. We can expect some similarity in the Territory key date behavior.

The Wisconsin high and low leaf varieties may prove to be rare enough to develop meaningful bottlenecks in the larger population over time. The high and low leaf varieties have an advantage over the extra tree issues in that they are very obvious. Notice that the high and low leaf issues have gone through the short term price spike and settled in at the roughly 25-40 percent off peak prices depending on grade. While its doubtful that any series can develop and hold 100 million adherents longer term especially considering the expected competition from the new 50 state parks quarters, Presidential dollars and Sacagawea dollars, we do know that the rarer die verities in dealer inventories has and will continue to drop substantially over time as we saw in the super coin inventory and time cycle.

Proof 50 States Quarters Clad	Mintage	PR-69 Prooof
1999-S Delaware	3,713,359	$8
1999-S Pennsylvania	3,713,359	$8
1999-S New Jersey	3,713,359	$8
1999-S Georgia	3,713,359	$8
1999-S Connecticut	3,713,359	$8
2000-S Massachusetts	4,020,172	$4
2000-S Maryland	4,020,172	$4
2000-S South Carolina	4,020,172	$4
2000-S New Hampshire	4,020,172	$4
2000-S Virginia	4,020,172	$4
2001-S New York	3,094,140	$6
2001-S North Carolina	3,094,140	$6
2001-S Rhode Island	3,094,140	$6
2001-S Vermont	3,094,140	$6
2001-S Kentucky	3,094,140	$6
2002-s Tennessee	3,084,245	$4
2002-S Ohio	3,084,245	$4
2002-S Louisiana	3,084,245	$4
2002-S Indiana	3,084,245	$4
2002-S Mississippi	3,084,245	$4
2003-S Illinois	3,408,516	$4
2003-S Alabama	3,408,516	$4
2003-S Maine	3,408,516	$4
2003-S Missouri	3,408,516	$4
2003-S Arkansas	3,408,516	$4
2004-S Michigan	2,740,684	$5
2004-S Florida	2,740,684	$5
2004-S Texas	2,740,684	$5
2004-S Iowa	2,740,684	$5
2004-S Wisconsin	2,740,684	$5
2005-S California	3,262,960	$4
2005-S Minnesota	3,262,960	$4
2005-S Oregon	3,262,960	$4
2005-S Kansas	3,262,960	$4
2005-S West Virginia	3,262,960	$4
2006-S Nevada	2,862,078	$4
2006-S Nebraska	2,862,078	$4
2006-S Colorado	2,862,078	$4

Proof 50 States Quarters Clad	Mintage	PR-69 Prooof
2006-S North Dakota	2,862,078	$4
2006-S South Dakota	2,862,078	$4
2007-S Idaho	2,374,778	$4
2007-S Montana	2,374,778	$4
2007-S Utah	2,374,778	$4
2007-S Washington	2,374,778	$4
2007-S Wyoming	2,374,778	$4
2008-S Oklahoma	2,100,000	$4
2008-S New Mexico	2,100,000	$4
2008-S Arizona	2,100,000	$4
2008-S Alaska	2,100,000	$4

Proof 50 States Quarters Silver	Mintage	PR-69 Prooof
1999-S Delaware	804,565	$65
1999-S Pennsylvania	804,565	$60
1999-S New Jersey	804,565	$60
1999-S Georgia	804,565	$60
1999-S Connecticut	804,565	$60
2000-S Massachusetts	965,421	$6
2000-S Maryland	965,421	$6
2000-S South Carolina	965,421	$6
2000-S New Hampshire	965,421	$6
2000-S Virginia	965,421	$6
2001-S New York	889,697	$25
2001-S North Carolina	889,697	$25
2001-S Rhode Island	889,697	$25
2001-S Vermont	889,697	$25
2001-S Kentucky	889,697	$25
2002-S Tennessee	892,229	$8
2002-S Ohio	892,229	$8
2002-S Louisiana	892,229	$8
2002-S Indiana	892,229	$8
2002-S Mississippi	892,229	$8
2003-S Illinois	1,257,555	$5
2003-S Alabama	1,257,555	$5
2003-S Maine	1,257,555	$5
2003-S Missouri	1,257,555	$5
2003-S Arkansas	1,257,555	$5

Proof 50 States Quarters Silver	Mintage	PR-69 Prooof
2004-S Michigan	1,775,370	$5
2004-S Florida	1,775,370	$5
2004-S Texas	1,775,370	$5
2004-S Iowa	1,775,370	$5
2004-S Wisconsin	1,775,370	$5
2005-S California	1,679,600	$5
2005-S Minnesota	1,679,600	$5
2005-S Oregon	1,679,600	$5
2005-S Kansas	1,679,600	$5
2005-S West Virginia	1,679,600	$5
2006-S Nevada	1,571,839	$5
2006-S Nebraska	1,571,839	$5
2006-S Colorado	1,571,839	$5
2006-S North Dakota	1,571,839	$5
2006-S South Dakota	1,571,839	$5
2007-S Idaho	1,299,878	$5
2007-S Montana	1,299,878	$5
2007-S Utah	1,299,878	$5
2007-S Washington	1,299,878	$5
2007-S Wyoming	1,299,878	$5
2008-S Oklahoma	1,200,000	$5
2008-S New Mexico	1,200,000	$5
2008-S Arizona	1,200,000	$5
2008-S Alaska	1,200,000	$5
2008-S Hawaii	1,200,000	$5

The characteristics of the 50 states silver proof quarters are reviewed extensively in the section entitled "The Dawn of the Changing Reverse Series" on page 38. They are the prototype for things to come.

Sacagawea—Native American Dollars

Mint State "Sac" Dollars

YEAR	MINTAGE	MS-63
2000-P	767,140,000	$2
2000-P Goodacre	5,000	$400
2000-P Detailed Feathers	5,500	$5,000
2000-D	518,916,000	$2
2001-P	62,468,000	$2
2001-D	70,939,500	$2
2002-P	3,865,610	$3
2002-D	3,732,000	$3
2003-P	3,080,000	$3
2003-D	3,080,000	$3
2004-P	2,660,000	$3
2004-D	2,660,000	$3
2005-P	2,520,000	$3
2005-D	2,520,000	$3
2006-P	4,900,000	$2
2006-D	2,800,000	$2
2007-P	3,640,000	$2
2007-D	3,920,000	$2
2008-P	9,800,000	$3
2008-D	14,840,000	$2
2009-P Three Sisters Rev	37,380,000	$2
2009-D Three Sisters Rev	33,880,000	$2

This series will have a great deal to teach us over the next 10 years. Like the 50 states quarter program, the Native American themed changing reverses will be added to a series that has been collected by date, mintmark, die variety and finish over the last eight years. The stable reverse coins issued from 2000 to 2008 have what look like two strong leaders in the 2000 Goodacre finish dollar and the so called Cheerios dollars with detailed tail feathers.

The Goodacre dollars were issued in payment to the designer of the new dollars and they were struck with a special finish. The coins were sent to the grading services and have "Goodacre" labels. Over the years the Mint has experimented with many different finishes in the hope of

improving the coin's retention of its "golden" color. The Goodacre dollar in effect is one of many finish variations, but it is a famous and recognized one.

2000-P Detailed Feathers

Very early in the Sacagawea dollar program, Cheerios ran a promotion that included a 2000 dated "golden dollar" in the box. It turns out that these coins were a die variety that has slightly different tail feather characteristics than the succeeding issues. There were only 5,500 coins in the Cheerios program to start with and most of those were spent into circulation shortly after issue. Very few high-grade examples of this die variety have survived and there is no question that as a variety, they are rarer than the Goodacre issues.

"Cheerios" dollars are very expensive in high grade.

One of the questions collectors of this set may wish to ask themselves is "Will the addition of the changing reverses help or hurt the relatively rare 2000 dated varieties?" Our study of the long-term price behavior of the proof silver quarters from 1936 to present would indicate that the Native American dollars could very well hurt the rarer back date's inflation adjusted values over time. Long-term inflation adjusted mint state Washington quarters behavior gives us some hope that if the influx of new collectors into this series is dramatic and the keys are rare enough the early stable design keys may escape the same fate as the type common but date rare 1939 P, D and S Arkansas commemorative halves whose 2,100 mintages could not propel them past $350 in mint state form after 70 years.

1935-1939
Arkansas P, D & S
Halves

Proof "Sac" Dollars

YEAR	MINTAGE
2000-S Eagle	4,048,000
2001-S Eagle	3,190,000
2002-S Eagle	3,210,000
2003-S Eagle	3,300,000
2004-S Eagle	2,965,000
2005-S Eagle	3,273,000
2006-S Eagle	3,028,828
2007-S Eagle	2,563,563
2008-S Eagle	
2009-S Three Sisters	

This proof series' greatest days are yet to come. The start of changing reverses in 2009 combined with the relatively free hand the Mint has been given in regard to design development is a good sign. This is one more inexpensive, easy to complete and attractive series that will effectively promote the "collector series" type concept.

Given that the Native American proof dollars, Presidential dollars and U.S. territory and state parks quarters will be issued together in proof sets from at least 2009 through 2016, it is likely that the collector bases will merge.

Presidential Dollars

Presidential Dollars- Basic Mint State and Proof

MINT STATE	MINTAGES		PROOFS	MINTAGE
	D	P		S
2007 Washington	163,680,000	176,680,000	2007 Washington	3,883,103
2007 Adams	112,140,000	112,420,000	2007 Adams	3,877,409
2007 Jefferson	102,810,000	100,800,000	2007 Jefferson	3,877,573
2007 Madison	87,780,000	84,560,000	2007 Madison	3,876,829
2008 Monroe	60,230,000	64,260,000	2008 Monroe	3,000,000
2008 Adams	57,720,000	57,540,000	2008 Adams	3,000,000
2008 Jackson	61,070,000	61,180,000	2008 Jackson	3,000,000
2008 Van Buren	50,960,000	51,520,000	2008 Van Buren	3,000,000
2009 Harrison	55,160,000	43,260,000	2009 Harrison	-
2009 Tyler	43,540,000	43,540,000	2009 Tyler	-
2009 Polk	41,720,000	46,620,000	2009 Polk	-
2009 Taylor	36,650,000	41,580,000	2009 Taylor	-

Mint State

These coins aren't by and large seeing circulation and mintages are huge so there aren't any date and mintmark scarce "key dates" worthy of mention prior to 2009 in common mint state grades. Presidential dollars grading higher than MS-66 however are very difficult to find even after Herculean searching and sorting efforts due to harsh initial manufacturing and transport processes. As a case in point one young collector named Justin Spivack who was awarded Young Numismatist of the Year in 2009 by PCGS for his work with this series screened or had submitted on his behalf in excess of 100,000 business strike Presidential dollars yielding just a dozen or so MS-68 specimens and a couple dozen of the scarcer MS-67 pieces where MS-67 is the finest known for that particular coin.

Issues coming out from 2009 on are likely to be seen in much lower numbers than the

2007-2008 dollars were because the Treasury is being inundated with a back flow of coinage from the public brought on by hardship. Treasury backflow induced low mintages compounded with a die variety or momentary series suspension other than Mint sets like the Sacs experienced from 2002 to 2007 would be a wonderful gift to this set.

This historically significant series is a study in modern variety collecting. The registry sets show distinctions by date, mintmark, finish, day of issue and edge varieties. By the time this series comes to a close there may be hundreds of varieties. Some serious collectors like Justin who pursue this series focus on the direction of the edge lettering plus the mintmarks. That alone translates into a 160 coin series by the time we reach the 40th president. Thankfully most of the varieties are quite obvious to the casual observer much like the 1955 double die cent.

Before buying the rarer high grade varieties and errors, take the time to do your homework about the probable final populations. *The trouble with variety and error collecting is we don't have a mintage table to give us some reasonable guide for eventual valuations. It's easy to get caught paying high premiums for special issues as soon as they come out just to find they are in fact common six months later.* Many enthusiasts got hurt by purchasing Washington smooth edge dollars for $300-$600, just to see them collapse back to the $50-$60 range a year later.

Proofs

Since proofs have much higher levels of quality control than their mint state siblings we can't reasonably expect varieties to play a large part in the series development. Hopefully, one of the issues will break out of the typical 2 million to 4 million coins range and give us a viable key before series closure. In any event, this historically significant series will build on and benefit from its stable reverse and changing obverse structure as previously described in the section called "The Dawn of the Changing Reverse Series" on page 38.

American Eagle Silver Dollars

American Eagle silver dollars are the modern equivalent to the Morgan dollar in many ways. Morgans were created by the Bland-Allison Act of 1878 to unitize the silver coming out of western mines even though the coins were not needed or wanted for circulation. As a result, about 380 million Morgans still survive today and are enjoyed by collectors for their high grade, large size, lovely design and high material content. Today's business issue silver dollars, the mint state silver Eagles, are also issued to unitize silver and are enjoyed by collectors for the same reasons.

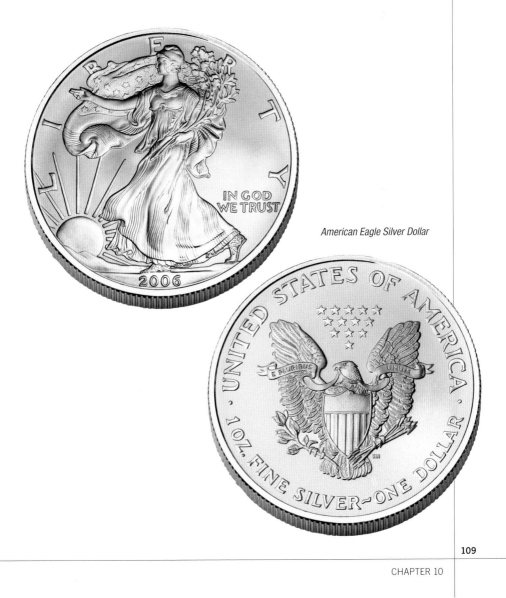

American Eagle Silver Dollar

1878 Morgan
Dollar

MINT STATE MORGAN DOLLARS		MS-63
	Mintage	Price
1878 8 feathers	750,000	$150
1878 7 feathers	9,759,550	$90
1878-CC	2,212,000	$290
1878-S	9,774,000	$65
1879	14,807,100	$50
1879-CC	756,000	$5,700
1879-O	2,887,000	$160
1879-S	9,110,000	$40
1879 - 78 reverse	In Above	$350
1880	12,601,335	$45
1880-CC	591,000	$530
1880-O	5,305,000	$300
1880-S	8,900,000	$40
1881	9,163,975	$50
1881-CC	296,000	$475
1881-O	5,708,000	$40
1881-S	12,760,000	$40
1882	11,101,000	$45
1882-CC	1,133,000	$200
1882-O	6,090,000	$50
1882-S	9,250,000	$45
1883	12,291,039	$40
1883-CC	1,204,000	$190
1883-O	8,725,000	$50
1883-S	6,250,000	$2,350
1884	14,070,875	$40
1884-CC	1,136,000	$200
1884-O	9,730,000	$40
1884-S	3,200,000	$26,000
FIRST 29 ISSUES	**189,600,000**	

MINT STATE SILVER EAGLE DOLLARS		MS-69
	Mintage	Price
1986	5,393,005	$22
1987	11,442,335	$20
1988	5,004,646	$20
1989	5,203,327	$20
1990	5,840,110	$20
1991	7,191,066	$20
1992	5,540,068	$20
1993	6,763,762	$20
1994	4,227,319	$20
1995	4,672,051	$22
1996	3,603,386	$40
1997	4,295,004	$25
1998	4,847,547	$20
1999	7,408,640	$20
2000	9,239,132	$20
2001	9,001,711	$20
2002	10,539,026	$20
2003	8,495,008	$20
2004	8,882,754	$20
2005	8,891,025	$20
2006	10,676,522	$20
2006-W	466,573	$70
2007	9,028,036	$20
2007-W	690,891	$25
2008	20,583,000	$20
2008-W	535,000 *	$25
2008-W 07 reverse	In above 47,000	$350
2009	30,459,500	$20
2009-W	None issued	
TOTAL POPULATION	**208,400,000**	

The above chart is comprised of the first 29 issues of both series, and it shows us several things:

1. Both series have massive total populations with most common dates running between 5 million and 20 million each.

2. At the current rate of production, the Eagles will match the surviving total Morgan population in the next 10 years.

3. In every case shown in the first 29 issues one mintmark stands dominant over the others. For the early Morgans it's the CC (Carson City) mintmark and for the silver Eagles it's the "W" (West Point) issues.

4. The typical common date Morgan shows a production run of about 7 million coins while the CC Morgans shown have an average run of 1 million coins.

5. The typical silver Eagle common date has an average of about 8 million coins struck per year and the consistently low mintage "W" issues are averaging only half a million coins a year.

The CC Morgans were not by and large issued to the public raw in rolls or bags, but in individual GSA packaging. GSA packaged CC Morgan populations look like this:

1878-CC	61,000
1879-CC	4,000
1880-CC	131,000
1881-CC	147,000
1882-CC	605,000
1883-CC	755,000
1884-CC	962,000
1885-CC	148,000

The "W" silver Eagles also were issued in individual government packaging while the common dates were shipped out by the thousands in rolls. Let's look at the "W" issues again:

2006-W	466,573
2007-W	690,891
2008-W	535,000*

Notice that the 1882, 1883 and 1884 CC coins are not the keys either to the CC set or the Morgan set, but the MS-63 issues that are the center of the population report grading bell line curve show a price of $200 each. The "W" silver Eagles are the keys to a 200 million and growing total population and have lower mintages than the surviving common date CC dollars and don't cost anything like $200 each yet. The "W" silver Eagles are the modern CC dollar and will likely have prices that reflect this reality over time.

There is one more similarity on the chart that is worthy of note. An 1879-S Morgan has a 1878 reverse just as the 2008-W has an issue with a 2007 reverse. Based on population reports, the 1879-S with the 78 reverse is as rare in mint state form as the 1879-CC is but it does not pull anything like the same price in the market place. This example shows clearly as does many others that die variety rarity is not as strong a form of product differentiation as mintmarks are. The 2008-W with the 07 reverse has a 47,000 coin mintage (according to a Freedom of Information Act request) and its listed in most coin publications and required in the registry sets. The extent to which these listings reinforce the perception that the 08-W/07 silver Eagle is needed for a complete date and mint mark set is the extent to which the coin will or will not appreciate from the current price levels.

If you think the silver Eagles set will be collected primarily by date and mint mark then this is what the set profile looks like without the 2008-W/2007 reverse die variety.

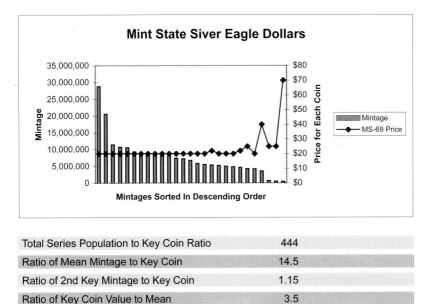

Total Series Population to Key Coin Ratio	444
Ratio of Mean Mintage to Key Coin	14.5
Ratio of 2nd Key Mintage to Key Coin	1.15
Ratio of Key Coin Value to Mean	3.5
Key Coin Price as Fraction of Whole Set	0.11

The old 1996 key date which has now been superceded by the three "W" issues has had 14 years to go through the dispersal process. This is why it trades for higher prices than the second and third place semi keys. This double horned structure is typical of under valued infants in the first three to five years after issue. The "W" mintmarked dollars in this set are badly undervalued.

Now let's look at the relative rarity price profile for this set with the 2008-W/2007 reverse added in.

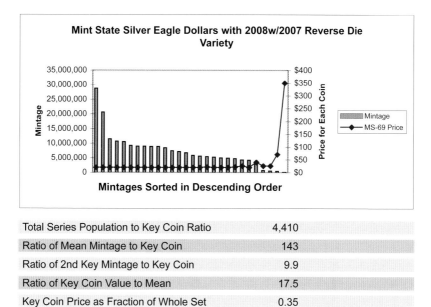

Total Series Population to Key Coin Ratio	4,410
Ratio of Mean Mintage to Key Coin	143
Ratio of 2nd Key Mintage to Key Coin	9.9
Ratio of Key Coin Value to Mean	17.5
Key Coin Price as Fraction of Whole Set	0.35

There is no question the 2008-W/2007 reverse silver Eagle has fantastic ratios. If the collectors who are working on the series by date and mintmark come to the conclusion that they must have one to complete their date and mintmark set the 08-W/07 has a bright future.

Proof Silver Eagle Dollars

Year	Mintages	PR-69 Price
1986	1,446,778	$45
1987	904,732	$45
1988	557,370	$45
1989	617,694	$45
1990	695,510	$45
1991	511,924	$45
1992	498,543	$50
1993	405,913	$80
1994	372,168	$105
1995	407,822	$100
1995-W	30,102	$3,000
1996	498,293	$70
1997	440,315	$75
1998	450,728	$55
1999	549,330	$55
2000	600,743	$45
2001	746,398	$45
2002	647,342	$45
2003	747,831	$45
2004	801,602	$45
2005	816,663	$45
2006	1,093,600	$45
2006-RP	248,875	$180
2007	821,759	$45
2008	700,979	$45
2009	None Issued	
TOTAL POPULATION =	**15,600,000**	

This massive proof silver dollar series needs no introduction. It's a perfect case study of why you need to see key dates before they drive the cost of the sets into the stratosphere. This coin is the modern proof Morgan. Notice that the sub half million mintage issues are starting to move into the $100 range. The 1992 and 1998 are undervalued assuming the mintage figures given to the public are correct.

See "Rare Coin Market Behavior" on page 28 for a detailed review of this series.

Modern Commemorative Halves

		MS-96
Year/Type- Mint State	**Mintage**	**Price**
1982-D Washington-Silver	2,210,458	$10
1986-D Statue of Liberty	928,008	$5
1989-D Bicentennial Congress	163,753	$7
1991-D Mount Rushmore	172,754	$18
1992-P Olympics Gymnast	161,607	$8
1992-D Columbus	135,702	$10
1993-W Bill of Rights-Silver	193,346	$16
1993-P World War II	197,072	$22
1994-D World Cup	168,208	$8
1995-S Basketball	171,001	$18
1995-S Baseball	164,605	$18
1995-S Civil War	119,510	$35
1996-S Soccer	52,836	$125
1996-S Swimming	49,533	$135
2001-P Capital Visitor Center	99,157	$12
2003-P First Flight	57,726	$12
2008-P Bald Eagle	120,000	$10

		PR-69
Year/Type - Proof	**Mintage**	**Price**
1982-S Washington-Silver	4,894,044	$10
1986-S Statue of Liberty	6,925,627	$7
1989-S Bicentennial Congress	762,198	$5
1991-S Mount Rushmore	753,257	$17
1992-S Olympics Gymnast	519,645	$8
1992-S Columbus	390,154	$10
1993-S Bill of Rights-Silver	586,315	$14
1993-P World War II	317,396	$23
1994-P World Cup	609,354	$7
1995-S Basketball	169,655	$15
1995-S Baseball	118,087	$16
1995-S Civil War	330,099	$35
1996-S Soccer	122,412	$90
1996-S Swimming	114,315	$30
2001-P Capital Visitor Center	77,962	$15
2003-P First Flight	109,710	$15
2008-P Bald Eagle	175,000	$12

These coins that populate the young collectors sets are an attractive type set. The mint state issues look well behaved as seen below.

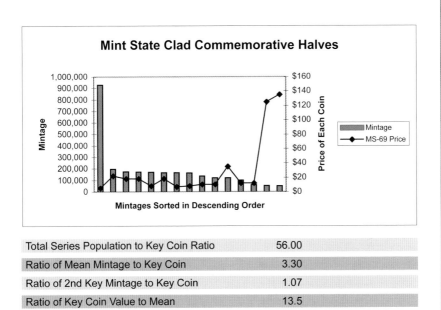

Total Series Population to Key Coin Ratio	56.00
Ratio of Mean Mintage to Key Coin	3.30
Ratio of 2nd Key Mintage to Key Coin	1.07
Ratio of Key Coin Value to Mean	13.5
Key Coin Price as Fraction of Whole Set	0.30

As we will see again in the proof silver commemorative dollars when type mintages are all fairly high, relative rarity among succeeding issues counts for very little. That said, the proof halves issued since 2000 look undervalued.

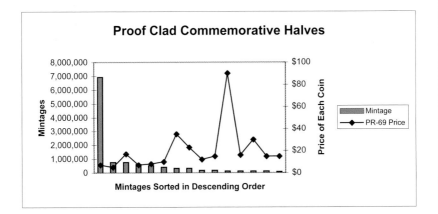

Proof Silver Dollar Commemoratives

Proof	Mintage	PR-69 Price
1983-S Discus	1,577,025	$18
1984-S Los Angeles	1,801,210	$18
1986-S Statue of Liberty	6,414,638	$18
1987-S Constitution	2,747,116	$18
1988-S Olympics	1,359,366	$18
1990-P Eisenhower	1,144,461	$18
1992-W White House	375,851	$18
1989-S Congress Bicentennial	762,198	$23
1991-P Korea	618,488	$18
1991-S Mount Rushmore	738,419	$21
1991S USO	321,275	$18
1992-P Columbus	385,241	$25
1992-W White House	375,849	$21
1992-S XXV Olympiad	504,505	$20
1993-S Bill of Rights	534,001	$18
1993-S Thomas Jefferson	332,891	$18
1993-W World War II	342,041	$34
1994-P POW	220,100	$36
1994-S US Capital	279,416	$24
1994-P Vietnam	226,262	$36
1994-P Women in Military	213,201	$27
1994-S World Cup	576,978	$21
1995-S Civil War	437,114	$62
1995-P Gymnastics	182,676	$44
1995-P Paralympics	138,337	$44
1995-P Special Olympics	351,764	$27
1995-P Track & Field	136,935	$44
1996-S Community Service	101,543	$68
1996P Cycling	118,795	$40
1996-P High Jump	124,502	$50
1996-P Rowing	151,890	$60
1996-P Smithsonian	129,152	$50
1996-P Tennis	92,016	$75
1996-P Wheel Chair	84,280	$72
1997-P Botanic Garden	264,528	$33
1997-S Jackie Robinson	110,495	$105
1997-P Law Enforcement	110,428	$90
1998-S Black War Patriot	75,070	$85
1998-S Robert Kennedy	99,020	$41
1999-P Dolley Madison	224,403	$30

Proof Silver Dollar Commemoratives continued

Proof	Mintage	PR-69 Price
1999-P Yellowstone	128,646	$40
2000-P Library of Congress	196,900	$30
2000-P Lief Ericson	144,748	$60
2001-P Buffalo	272,869	$165
2001-P Capital Visitor Center	143,793	$35
2002-P Salt Lake City	166,864	$35
2002-W West Point	288,293	$16
2003-P First Flight	193,086	$26
2004-P Edison	213,409	$30
2004-P Lewis & Clark	288,492	$20
2005-P John Marshall	141,993	$30
2005-P Marine	548,810	$42
2006-P Franklin Founding	136,037	$38
2006-P Franklin Scientist	137,808	$38
2006-S San Francisco	255,700	$38
2007-P Desegregation	124,678	$31
2007-P Jamestown	258,802	$31
2008-P Bald Eagle	243,558	$35
2009-P Braille	* 135,000	$35
2009-P Lincoln	* 375,000	$55
TOTAL POPULATION=	**29,000,000**	

The proof silver dollar commemoratives series makes for a very attractive set with over 50 oz of silver backing your $2,000 to $3,000 expenditure. As you can see below, the mintage vs. price profile for this set possesses a great deal of "noise" and it lacks a strong key to lead it. None of the coins in the set are particularly scarce nor is relative rarity among members all that important, so the most expensive issue is the very common but ever popular Buffalo dollar.

This set's classic forerunner, the silver commemoratives halves, sheds a great deal of light on the behavior of this set. See the "Unstable Design Models and Type Coin Market Dynamics" section on page 33 for a detailed review of this series structure.

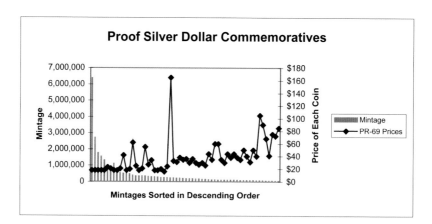

Total Series Population to Key Coin Ratio	389
Ratio of Mean Mintage to Key Coin	3.8
Ratio of 2nd Key Mintage to Key Coin	1.1
Ratio of Key Coin Value to Mean	2.4
Key Coin Price as Fraction of Whole Set	0.04

Mint State Commemorative Dollars

Proof	Mintage	MS-69 Price
1983-P Los Angeles	294,543	$18
1983-D Los Angeles	174,014	$18
1983-S Los Angeles	174,014	$18
1984-P Olympic	217,954	$18
1984-D Olympic	116,675	$18
1984-S Olympic	116,675	$18
1986-P Statue of Liberty	723,635	$18
1987-P Constitution	451,629	$18
1988-D Olympiad	191,368	$18
1989-D Congress	135,203	$20
1990-W Eisenhower	241,669	$18
1991-P Mount Rushmore	133,139	$25
1991-D Korean War	213,049	$18
1991-D USO	124,958	$20
1992-D XXV Olympiad	187,552	$20
1992-D Columbus	106,949	$20
1992-D White House	123,803	$22
1993-D Bill of Rights	98,383	$20
1993-D WWII	94,708	$26
1994-D World Cup	81,698	$20
1993-P Jefferson Silver	266,927	$18
1994-W Vietnam	57,317	$70
1994-W POW	54,790	$70
1994-W Women Service	53,054	$33
1994-D Capital	68,352	$20
1995-P Civil War	45,866	$62
1995-D Gymnastics	42,497	$60
1995-D Paralympics	28,649	$74
1995-D Track and Field	24,976	$70
1995-D Cycling	19,662	$125
1995-W Special Olympics	89,301	$26
1996-D Tennis	15,983	$270
1996-D High Jump	15,697	$330
1996-D Wheelchair	14,497	$320
1996-D Rowing	16,258	$300
1996-S Community Service	23,500	$180
1996-D Smithsonian	31,230	$110
1997-P Botanic Garden	57,272	$35
1997-S Jackie Robinson	30,007	$82
1997-P Law Enforcement	28,575	$140

continued next page

Mint State Commemorative Dollars continued

Proof	Mintage	MS-69 Price
1998-S Robert Kennedy	106,422	$33
1998-S Black Patriots	37,210	$130
1999-P Dolly Madison	89,104	$37
1999-P Yellowstone	23,614	$44
2000-P Library Of Congress	52,771	$35
2000-P Leif Erickson	28,150	$75
2001-D American Buffalo	227,100	$140
2001-P Visitor Center	35,400	$28
2002-P Salt Lake City	40,257	$27
2002-W West Point	103,201	$20
2003-P First Flight	53,761	$30
2004-P Thomas Edison	68,051	$34
2004-P Lewis and Clark	90,323	$21
2005-P John Marshall	48,953	$28
2005-P Marine Corps	49,671	$32
2006-P Franklin-Scientist	61,956	$24
2006-P Franklin-Founder	64,014	$25
2006-S San Francisco	65,609	$35
2007-P Central High	66,093	$30
2007-P Jamestown	79,801	$30
2008-P Bald Eagle	110,073	$28
2009-P Lincoln	* 125,000	$55
2009-P Braille	* 83,000	$35

TOTAL SERIES POPULATION=6,700,000   **COMPLETE SET=$4,000**

This attractive and interesting set is composed of well over 50 coins and many of them are very low mintage for U.S. silver dollars. *The 1996 mint state silver dollar commemoratives issued with sub 16,000 mintages are the rarest silver dollars issued since the great depression.*

On the surface some of the members of this set look cheap for the mintage range they inhabit. It's useful to look for good historical reference points that can give you some idea if a series you are interested in has reached full maturity or not. Note that the1935 Old Spanish Trail and Hudson commemorative halves are among the three lead coins in their series with 10,000 coin mintages and they bring about $1,000-$1,400 each in typical mint state grades after over 70 years. It's likely that barring strong marketing intervention the 15,000 mintage 1996 Olympic commemorative dollars will top out somewhere short of the prices reached by their 10,000 mintage forefathers.

Commemoratives and their behavior are covered at length in the section titled "Unstable Design Models and Type Coin Market Dynamics" on page 33. Below is the relative rarity price profile for mint state silver dollar commemoratives.

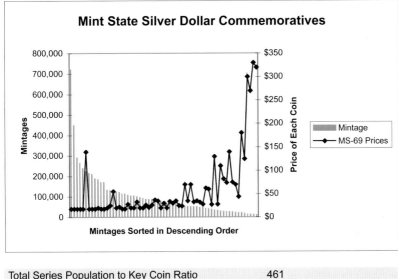

Total Series Population to Key Coin Ratio	461
Ratio of Mean Mintage to Key Coin	4.7
Ratio of 2nd Key Mintage to Key Coin	1.1
Ratio of Key Coin Value to Mean	10.7
Key Coin Price as Fraction of Whole Set	0.09

1996 Wheelchair   1997 Jackie Robinson Dollar

Mint State $5 Gold Commemoratives

	Mintage	MS-69 Price
1986 $5 MS Liberty Gold	95,248	$325
1987 $5 MS Constitution Gold	214,225	$325
1988 $5 MS Olympiad Gold	62,913	$325
1989 $5 MS Congress Gold	46,899	$325
1991 $5 MS Rushmore Gold	31,139	$375
1992 $5 MS Olympiad Gold	27,732	$375
1992 $5 MS Columbus Gold	24,329	$375
1993 $5 MS Bill of Rights Gold	23,266	$400
1993 $5 MS World War II Gold	23,089	$425
1994 $5 MS World Cup Gold	22,464	$350
1995 $5 MS Civil War Gold	12,735	$900
1995 $5 MS Torch Runner Gold	14,675	$850
1995 $5 MS Stadium Gold	10,579	$2,000
1996 $5 MS Flag Gold	9,174	$2,000
1996 $5 MS Cauldron Gold	9,210	$2,000
1996 $5 MS Smithsonian Gold	9,068	$850
1997 $5 MS Jackie R. Gold	5,174	$4,000
1997 $5 MS FDR Gold	11,894	$1,500
1999 $5 MS Washington Gold	22,511	$400
2001 $5 MS Visitor Center Gold	6,761	$1,600
2002 $5 MS Salt Lake Gold	10,585	$400
2006 $5 MS Old Mint Gold	16,230	$350
2007 $5 MS Jamestown Gold	18,843	$350
2008 $5 MS Bald Eagle Gold	13,467	$350

COMPLETE SET PRICE = $21,000
SET'S INTRINSIC VALUE= $6,000 AT $1,000 GOLD.

2001 Capital Visitor
$5 Gold

From the mid-1990s until 2004 this series was the only modern series worthy of note in terms of significant type coin rarity. Strong market makers took notice and began the long process of promoting the keys. As a result this set has experienced a dramatic reduction in the time it normally takes for a series to reach full maturity. Its once immature keys have seen a five to 15 fold increase over the last seven to 10 years. While this set may not be over valued, it has become expensive and its growth rate is going to see a dramatic reduction from now on.

Looking back through coinage history 5,000-6,000 population type coins are not normally worth much more than $5,000 long term. This series is running out of space to grow unless it is artificially forced up and if that's the case the cornering party will be taking on unnecessary exit risk.

The $5 mint state commemoratives relative rarity price profile and ratios are below. This set's lack of a stable design element coupled with the influence of promotional efforts by strong maketers on a few specific issues has produced the obvious distortion in the sets price profile. See the section titled "Unstable Design Models" on page 33.

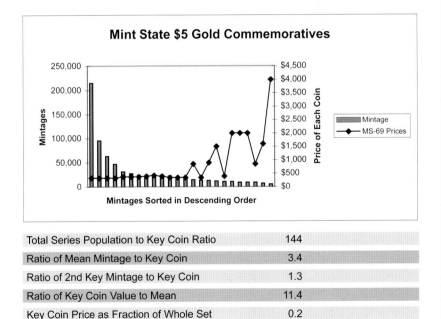

Total Series Population to Key Coin Ratio	144
Ratio of Mean Mintage to Key Coin	3.4
Ratio of 2nd Key Mintage to Key Coin	1.3
Ratio of Key Coin Value to Mean	11.4
Key Coin Price as Fraction of Whole Set	0.2

$5 Proof Gold Commemoratives

Proof	Mintage	Price PR-69
1986 Statue of Liberty $5 Gold	404,013	$325
1987 Constitution $5 Gold	651,659	$325
1988 Olympiad $5 Gold	281,465	$325
1989 Congress Bic. $5 Gold	164,690	$325
1991 Mount Rushmore $5 Gold	111,991	$325
1992 XXV Olympiad $5 Gold	77,313	$325
1992 Columbus $5 Gold	79,730	$325
1993 Bill of Rights $5 Gold	78,651	$325
1993 World War II $5 Gold	65,461	$325
1994 World Cup $5 Gold	89,614	$325
1995 Civil War $5 Gold	55,246	$375
1995 Torch Runner $5 Gold	57,442	$335
1995 Stadium $5 Gold	43,124	$520
1996 Flag Bearer $5 Gold	32,886	$580
1996 Cauldron $5 Gold	38,555	$525
1996 Smithsonian $5 Gold	21,840	$500
1997 Jackie Robinson $5 Gold	24,072	$525
1997 Roosevelt $5 Gold	29,233	$325
1999 Washington $5 Gold	41,693	$330
2001 Capital Visitor $5 Gold	27,652	$380
2002 Salt Lake $5 Gold	32,877	$325
2006 San Francisco Mint $5	41,517	$325
2007 Jamestown $5 Gold	47,050	$325
2008 Bald Eagle $5 Gold	59,000	$325

COMPLETE SET PRICE = $9,000
SET'S INTRINSIC VALUE= $6,000 AT $1,000 GOLD.

2007
Jamestown
$5 Gold

The set is attractive but like most of the proof gold Eagle denominations it desperately needs a strong key to give it leadership. The set is low risk and still has some room to grow. This type set shows the typical pricing wander expected from an unstable design model. See the section titled "Unstable Design Models" on page 33.

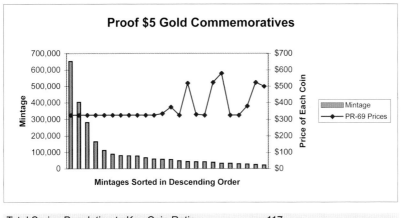

Proof $5 Gold Commemoratives

Total Series Population to Key Coin Ratio	117
Ratio of Mean Mintage to Key Coin	2.6
Ratio of 2nd Key Mintage to Key Coin	1.1
Ratio of Key Coin Value to Mean	1.5
Key Coin Price as Fraction of Whole Set	0.05

2008 Bald
Eagle $5
Gold

2002 Salt Lake
$5 Gold

Mint State Gold Eagles

$5 Mint State Gold Eagles

Year	Mintage	MS-69 Price
1986	912,609	$140
1987	580,266	$140
1988	159,500	$200
1989	264,790	$140
1990	210,210	$140
1991	165,200	$150
1992	209,300	$140
1993	210,709	$140
1994	206,380	$140
1995	223,025	$140
1996	401,964	$140
1997	528,515	$140
1998	1,344,520	$140
1999	2,750,338	$140
1999-W	6,000*	$500
2000	569,153	$140
2001	269,147	$140
2002	230,027	$140
2003	245,029	$140
2004	250,016	$140
2005	300,043	$140
2006	285,006	$140
2006-W	20,643	$150
2007	190,010	$130
2007-W	22,501	$150
2008	305,000	$130
2008-W	12,657	$200
2009	270,000*	$140
TOTAL MINTAGE =	**11,142,000**	

The $5 gold Eagles set is the most affordable and completable of all U.S. gold coin series. When you consider that the quarter eagle Indian set is its closest antique equivalent and costs about $35,000 for a MS-63 set, the $5 gold Eagles MS-69 $4,000 complete set price tag is attractive.

As has been seen previously, massive total series populations are silent advertisements for the series and this set's total population has already exceeded that of the similar sized classic quarter Eagle gold Indians. The U.S. Mint gave this set a much needed gift when it struck a series of four "W" mintmarked gold Eagles with mintages at least seven times rarer than the next closest nonmintmarked issue.

These four mint state West Point mintmarked coins pictured above have been given interesting titles. The 2006, 2007 and 2008 coins were struck on standard blanks that were rolled in the presence of small metal balls and then struck with unfinished "W" mintmarked proof dies. The coins were called "burnished uncirculated" as opposed to American Eagle gold bullion coins so that they could be marketed directly to the public instead of having to go through the dealer network for typical mint state finish coins even though that's exactly what they look like.

In 1999, in the midst of the Y2K gold buying panic, West Point mint production exploded forcing lax quality control and either intentionally or unintentionally unpolished proof dies were used to strike a few "W" mintmarked issues very late in the year. The 1999-W gold Eagles were given the title "error" coins even though there is nothing out of the ordinary except the presence of a "W" mintmark.

It is highly likely that the number of complete date and mint-marked sets of these beautiful little coins will be limited by the mint-age of the 1999-W. According to the Office of Public Affairs, the Mint expects to change out the dies for this program about every 6,000 coins. This may prove to be a helpful reference point.

The combined population report for these relatively expensive coins stood at 2,600 coins in the fall of 2005. That's about 430 coins per year submitted. Since then submissions have fallen to 350 coins per year and a grand total of 4,000 $5 coins have shown up to be graded since early in 2000. Very few new raw rolls have been showing up in the marketplace lately and many of the new submissions are resubmits because softer grading standards give previously graded MS-69 coins a reasonable chance at making 70.

Looking back through coinage history it's hard to find series with high grade populations this huge with key date mintages in the 6,000-22,000 coin range to use as a solid mature reference point for long-term behavior. That said, if the series continues on to its end without any more mintmarked coins, then all the $5 "W" issues should reward their owners handsomely. If this inexpensive, attractive, and completeable gold series becomes popular, the 1999-W could easily trade for $2,000 each in high grade because it is to this set what the 1911-D is to the quarter Eagle gold Indians.

MODERN COMMEMORATIVE COINS

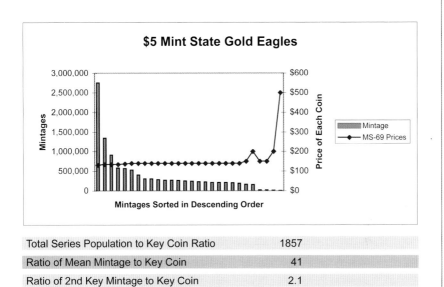

$5 Mint State Gold Eagles

Mintages Sorted in Descending Order

Total Series Population to Key Coin Ratio	1857
Ratio of Mean Mintage to Key Coin	41
Ratio of 2nd Key Mintage to Key Coin	2.1
Ratio of Key Coin Value to Mean	3.6
Key Coin Price as Fraction of Whole Set	0.11

Note the mintage of the 1999-W is so small scaled to its siblings it doesn't even show up.

The fourth place 1988 has had 22 years to mature and that creates the slight double horn structure that indicates the semi key "W" issues are undervalued as a result of their youth.

The Mint posted this comment on its Web site in mid-2009:

"As a result of the recent numismatic product portfolio analysis, fractional sizes of American Eagle Gold Uncirculated Coins will no longer be produced."

The uncirculated coins referred to are the "W" mintmarked fractional gold Eagles. As Solomon once said, ***"The end of a thing is better than the beginning of a thing" and that certainly applies to low mintage mintmarked gold if you pick them up before they mature.***

$10 Mint State Gold Eagles

Year	Mintage	MS-69 Price
1986	726,031	$325
1987	269,255	$325
1988	49,000	$325
1989	81,789	$325
1990	41,000	$375
1991	36,100	$400
1992	59,546	$325
1993	71,864	$325
1994	72,650	$325
1995	83,752	$325
1996	60,318	$325
1997	108,805	$325
1998	309,829	$325
1999	564,232	$325
1999-W	<6,000*	$1,000
2000	128,964	$325
2001	71,280	$325
2002	62,027	$325
2003	74,029	$325
2004	72,014	$325
2005	72,015	$325
2006	60,004	$325
2006-W	15,188	$500
2007	34,004	$325
2007-W	12,766	$500
2008	70,000*	$325
2008-W	8,883	$800
2009	110,000*	$325
TOTAL MINTAGE =	**3,325,000**	

Like its smaller denomination $5 siblings the complete $10 gold Eagle sets offer high material content as a percentage of purchase price and four outstanding low mintage key dates rare enough to develop pronounced bottlenecks in the large total population.

The "W" mintmarked gold eagles from 2006, 2007 and 2008 have already gained the attention of market makers with strong hands. The three later "W" issues are common enough to take a sizable position in but rare enough to make cornering the market an achievable task. These coins are desirable and may reach price maturity much faster than one would normally expect based solely on typical collector base growth rates. They are pictured above with their 1999-W sibling.

The 1999-W $10 gold Eagles were struck under the same circumstances as their $5 sibling but fewer of them are showing up in the combined population reports from NGC and PCGS. There are very few dealers that inventory these coins and fresh raw rolls over the last two years have been almost nonexistent (a little over 100 coins in over two years). Most growth in the population reports as small as they are have been from attractive previously submitted coins being cracked out of their holders and resubmitted in hopes of grading higher under the current, much more lenient, standards.

We know that the budgeted change-out rate on the dies for this program is listed as 6,000 coins per die set. So far only about 2,300 $10 1999-W gold Eagles have shown up in the combined NGC and PCGS reports including resubmits. This begs the question: If the $5 and $10 gold Eagles both were each run for one set of dies then why are there significantly more $5 coins than there are $10 coins? One likely explanation is the Mint in this period was striking on average 7,500 $5 coins a day but just 1,500 $10 gold Eagles. It is completely possible that the $5 dies were run beyond the Mint's expected average while the larger coins were not. It is also possible that the $10 dies were damaged and taken out of service early. An entire roll of the 1999-W gold Eagle quarters showed up at PCGS with obvious identical die damage on Miss Liberty's leg.

Fred Weinberg, who actively researched both of the fractional 1999-W issues at the time of their release, found that some of the coins were sent to jewelry fabricators in Asia. It's a process that's not kind to high-grade moderns.

There is little doubt that the 1999-W is the key to the entire fractional gold Eagle series and is the rarest fractional gold coin issued to the public since FDR suspended gold coinage production in 1933. Like so many things in life we will not know the fate of the 1999-W gold quarter until after the fact, but ***it looks like this coin will be to this set what the 1909-O is to the half eagle Indians***.

This set's total population is huge and its four keys are such tight bottlenecks that complete date and mintmark sets may be very expensive in the out years. The 1999-W, 2006-W, 2007-W and 2008-W all model well.

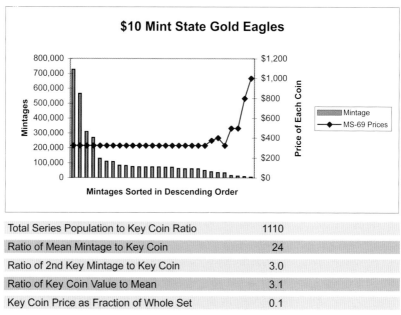

Total Series Population to Key Coin Ratio	1110
Ratio of Mean Mintage to Key Coin	24
Ratio of 2nd Key Mintage to Key Coin	3.0
Ratio of Key Coin Value to Mean	3.1
Key Coin Price as Fraction of Whole Set	0.1

$25 Mint State Gold Eagles

Year	Mintage	MS-69 Price
1986	599,566	$600
1987	131,255	$700
1988	45,000	$790
1989	44,829	$850
1990	31,000	$900
1991	24,100	$1,600
1992	54,404	$700
1993	73,324	$600
1994	62,400	$600
1995	53,474	$700
1996	39,287	$700
1997	79,605	$600
1998	169,029	$600
1999	263,013	$600
1999-W	None	
2000	79,287	$600
2001	48,047	$650
2002	70,027	$600
2003	79,029	$600
2004	98,040	$600
2005	80,023	$600
2006	66,005	$600
2006-W	15,164	$975
2007	47,002	$600
2007-W	11,455	$1,000
2008	61,000	$600
2008-W	15,683	$975
2009	110,000	$600
TOTAL POPULATION =	**2,451,000**	

There are many good reasons to like this series other than its good looks and high material content.

This series older issue's prices have already started to "stretch out" from the common dates. The 1991 issue reigned as the undisputed key to this gold Eagle denomination for 15 years and as it went through the maturation process it became the darling of several institutional coin dealers including those that buy for retirement programs.

Some dealers suggest that the 1991 and 1990 $25 gold Eagles are the real keys to this set because they were not appreciated in their infancy and they experience grade deterioration. The 1991 gold Eagle was already trading safely over melt by 1995 so if the members of the issue were mistreated it would have had to occur over a very short window of time. The point is the older 1990-1991 keys have moved from first to fourth place in the mintage ranking and their only hope of continued dominance is some combination of condition rarity, continued institutional buying and the head start they have on finding stable homes.

The 2007-W is likely to pull past the value of the 1991 in the next 10 years and it is very fortunate to not have direct competition from a 1999-W. This is the most pronounced "double horned" price structure in modern numismatics. Look at how much more expensive the 1991 $25 gold is than the dramatically rarer "W" mintmarked issues from 2006-2008 are. As the West Point keys go through the absorption process outlined on the chart labeled "Super Coin Market Inventory" shown on page 49 we can expect the young keys to supercede the much more common predecessors from the early 1990s.

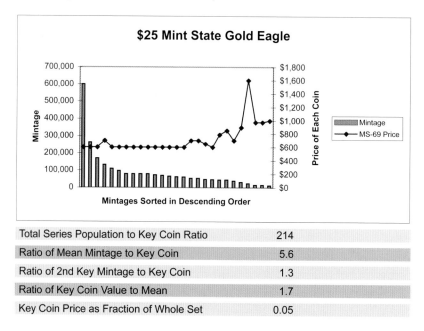

Total Series Population to Key Coin Ratio	214
Ratio of Mean Mintage to Key Coin	5.6
Ratio of 2nd Key Mintage to Key Coin	1.3
Ratio of Key Coin Value to Mean	1.7
Key Coin Price as Fraction of Whole Set	0.05

$50 Mint State Gold Eagles

Year	Mintage	MS-69 Price
1986	1,362,650	$1,200
1987	1,045,500	$1,200
1988	465,500	$1,200
1989	415,790	$1,200
1990	373,219	$1,200
1991	243,100	$1,200
1992	275,000	$1,200
1993	480,192	$1,200
1994	221,663	$1,200
1995	200,636	$1,200
1996	189,148	$1,200
1997	664,508	$1,200
1998	1,468,530	$1,200
1999	1,505,026	$1,200
1999-W	-	
2000	433,319	$1,200
2001	143,605	$1,200
2002	222,029	$1,200
2003	416,032	$1,200
2004	417,149	$1,200
2005	356,555	$1,200
2006	237,510	$1,200
2006-W	45,912	$1,250
2007	140,016	$1,200
2007-W	18,609	$1,300
2008	710,000	$1,200
2008-W	11,908	$1,450
2009	* 1,315,500	$1,200
TOTAL MINTAGE =	**13,400,000**	

This series has been the Mint's workhorse bullion issue for 24 years. Its typical production run is over a quarter of a million coins and until recently it didn't have any known keys worthy of note. That changed in 2008.

The high material prices and a worldwide shortage of processed blanks for coinage more than likely contributed to the 2008-W's relatively low mintage. This set clearly needed published keys with dramatically lower mintage than the common dates and now it looks like it finally has them.

For those who like to collect a series that offers no risk other than the fluctuation in the price of gold this is it. The presence of the three "W" mintmarked issues give the set some badly needed numismatic flair that it lacked before. The 2008-W and 2007-W have lovely ratios and likely a bright future to go with it.

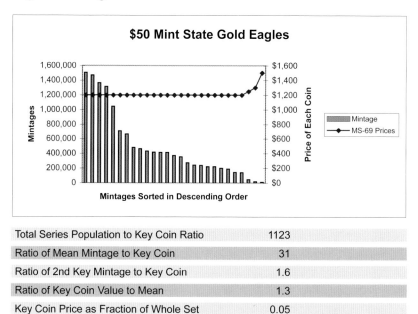

Total Series Population to Key Coin Ratio	1123
Ratio of Mean Mintage to Key Coin	31
Ratio of 2nd Key Mintage to Key Coin	1.6
Ratio of Key Coin Value to Mean	1.3
Key Coin Price as Fraction of Whole Set	0.05

Proof Gold Eagles

$5 Proof Gold Eagles

Year	Mintage	PR-69 Price
1988	143,881	$200
1989	84,647	$200
1990	99,349	$200
1991	70,334	$200
1992	64,874	$200
1993	45,960	$200
1994	62,849	$200
1995	62,667	$200
1996	57,047	$200
1997	34,977	$200
1998	39,395	$200
1999	48,428	$200
2000	49,971	$200
2001	37,530	$200
2002	40,864	$200
2003	40,027	$200
2004	35,131	$200
2005	49,265	$200
2006	47,277	$200
2007	58,553	$200
2008	28,116	$200
2009	none	
TOTAL MINTAGE =	**1,200,000**	

This lovely little set has done nothing more than track bullion prices over the last 20 years because it didn't have a key date with enough rarity to catch the attention of collectors or produce any meaningful bottle necks in the series. The series has finally started selling at a descent premium over melt because of a proof gold promotion that got started around the first of the year in 2009.

The new key to this set that arrived in 2008 with its 28,116 mintage is the current key of a 1.2 million population. If the 2008 endures as the key date longer term and its siblings continue their habit of selling well over 35,000 coins every year, the 2008 may do very well. If we see several years of sub 35,000 mintages, the 2008's hope of attaining serious key date status will be lost due to dilution of its shallow mintage advantage.

Total Series Population to Key Coin Ratio	43
Ratio of Mean Mintage to Key Coin	1.75
Ratio of 2nd Key Mintage to Key Coin	1.25
Ratio of Key Coin Value to Mean	1
Key Coin Price as Fraction of Whole Set	0.05

$10 Proof Gold Eagles

Year	Mintage	PR-69 Price
1988	98,028	$500
1989	54,170	$500
1990	62,674	$500
1991	50,839	$500
1992	46,269	$500
1993	33,775	$500
1994	48,172	$500
1995	47,526	$500
1996	38,219	$500
1997	29,805	$500
1998	29,503	$500
1999	34,417	$500
2000	36,036	$500
2001	25,613	$500
2002	29,242	$500
2003	30,292	$500
2004	28,839	$500
2005	37,207	$500
2006	36,127	$500
2007	46,189	$500
2008	18,877	$500
2009	none	
TOTAL MINTAGE =	**862,000**	

This lovely proof gold set's members have moved from trading at 20 percent over the melt value of its gold in January 2009 to two to three times melt by December 2009 due to a widespread proof gold promotion by dealers who serve IRA participants. With the exception of the 2008 issue, all the members of this set are high mintage and trade at the same price regardless of relative rarity status. ***Paying over twice melt for the common dates of this series is a very risky proposition.***

The current key to this denominational set the 2008 issue shows a mintage of 18,877 coins, but this data is suspect. The final weekly sales report showed that 28,000 coins sold. A Mint report issued in early 2009 in response to a Freedom of Information Act request shows 29,417 of them were struck. Proof gold's scrap rate is normally very stable at around 15 percent. The bottom line is in order for the 2008 $10 proof gold to be a 18,877 mintage coin, the weekly sales report had to be high by 10,000 coins and the scrap rate on that particular issue would need be about 35 percent.

Assuming the U.S. Mint mintage report dated Sept. 30, 2009, is correct, the 2008 $10 gold proof has a mintage of 18,877, and its by far the best this denomination has to offer. Only the 2006 $50 Reverse Proof Anniversary Gold Eagle is stronger among all proof gold eagles regardless of denomination.

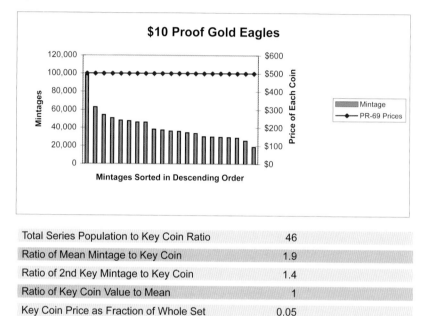

Total Series Population to Key Coin Ratio	46
Ratio of Mean Mintage to Key Coin	1.9
Ratio of 2nd Key Mintage to Key Coin	1.4
Ratio of Key Coin Value to Mean	1
Key Coin Price as Fraction of Whole Set	0.05

$25 Proof Gold Eagles

Year	Mintage	PR-69 Price
1987	143,398	$1,000
1988	76,528	$1,000
1989	44,798	$1,000
1990	51,636	$1,000
1991	53,125	$1,000
1992	40,976	$1,000
1993	31,130	$1,000
1994	44,584	$1,000
1995	45,388	$1,000
1996	35,058	$1,000
1997	26,344	$1,000
1998	25,374	$1,000
1999	30,427	$1,000
2000	32,028	$1,000
2001	23,240	$1,000
2002	26,646	$1,000
2003	28,270	$1,000
2004	27,330	$1,000
2005	34,311	$1,000
2006	34,322	$1,000
2007	44,025	$1,000
2008	22,602	$1,000
2009	none	
TOTAL MINTAGE =	**920,000**	

Unfortunately, this series needs a deep key to create collector interest and meaningful bottlenecks in the population. If you are going to buy a $25 proof gold Eagle for your collection, it might as well be the 2008 half with its 22,602 mintage.

This set's members have moved from trading at 1.2 times the melt value of its gold in January 2009 to two to three times melt by December 2009 due to a widespread proof gold promotion by dealers who serve IRA participants. Paying over twice melt for the common dates of this series is a very risky proposition.

$25 Proof Gold Eagles

Total Series Population to Key Coin Ratio	41
Ratio of Mean Mintage to Key Coin	1.5
Ratio of 2nd Key Mintage to Key Coin	1.03
Ratio of Key Coin Value to Mean	1
Key Coin Price as Fraction of Whole Set	0.05

2006 $50 Reverse Proof Gold Eagle

$50 Proof Gold Eagles

Year	Mintage	PR-69 Price
1986	446,290	$2,000
1987	147,498	$2,000
1988	87,133	$2,000
1989	54,570	$2,000
1990	62,401	$2,000
1991	50,411	$2,000
1992	44,826	$2,000
1993	34,369	$2,000
1994	46,674	$2,000
1995	46,368	$2,000
1996	36,153	$2,000
1997	28,034	$2,000
1998	25,886	$2,000
1999	31,427	$2,000
2000	33,007	$2,000
2001	24,555	$2,000
2002	27,499	$2,000
2003	28,344	$2,000
2004	28,215	$2,000
2005	35,246	$2,000
2006	47,000	$2,000
2006RP	9,996	$2,800
2007	51,810	$2,000
2008	30,237	$2,000
2009	none	
TOTAL MINTAGE =	**1,457,000**	

The 20th anniversary $50 reverse proof is dramatically rarer than its strongest siblings and has good ratios. The limiting factor for this set is the cost barrier to entry associated with the gold. Fewer and fewer collectors have the willingness and capacity to pursue a set as its price increases. *In theory it would take about one-half billion dollars to absorb 10,000 complete $50 proof gold sets as of this writing.* By comparison it requires about $20 million to absorb 6,000 $5 mint state gold Eagle sets. The bottom line is the $50 proof series will help drive the $50 reverse proof to some extent, but that alone may not be enough.

It will be interesting to see how the various collector bases converge on this set's reverse proof key. Those who hold 20th anniversary silver sets, 10th anniversary gold sets and 10th anniversary platinum sets would likely be interested even if they chose not to pursue the $50 proof gold denomination. Modern type collectors may come to regard the three-coin 20th anniversary set as the ideal modern gold Eagle $50 type set.

There are plenty of outstanding 10,000 mintage classic and modern coins in the marketplace and they have a hard time pulling past about $3,000 each. Collector base convergence or a very well financed promotion may be needed to drive the 2006 reverse proof well past its current price range. At the time of this writing there is an aggressive promotion impacting the market prices of the common date issues of this set, and they are extremely high risk when purchased at over twice intrinsic value.

Total Series Population to Key Coin Ratio	146
Ratio of Mean Mintage to Key Coin	3.6
Ratio of 2nd Key Mintage to Key Coin	2.5
Ratio of Key Coin Value to Mean	1.4
Key Coin Price as Fraction of Whole Set	0.06

Buffalo Gold and Silver

This very popular design that is identical to type one Buffalo nickels has now been struck in five modern mint state and proof denominations.

Proof Buffalo Mintages Gold and Silver

Year	$50	$25	$10	$5	$1
2001		-	-	-	272,869
2006	246,267	-	-	-	-
2007	58,998	-	-	-	-
2008	18,863	12,169	13,125	18,884	-
2009	50,000+	*	-	-	-
TOTAL=375,000*				**+ESTIMATE**	

Mint State Buffalo Mintages Gold and Silver

Year	$50	$25	$10	$5	$1
2001		-	-	-	227,131
2006	337,012	-	-	-	-
2007	136,503	-	-	-	-
2008	189,500	-	-	-	-
2008-W	9,074	16,908	9,949	17,429	-
2009	200,000	-	-	-	-
TOTAL=870,000*					

The popularity of this design is hard to overstate. As we covered before, the Buffalo silver dollars are one of the most common silver dollar commemoratives ever struck, but they are also one of the most expensive. If a quarter of a million mintage silver dollar is worth $150 each after they have had nine years to mature, where does that put these 10,000-20,000 mintage gold fractional type coins? If the Mint refrains from making any more fractional gold Buffaloes, the prices on these coins have very bright prospects.

Most of the world has gone to .999 pure gold issues. As a result, the 90 percent pure American Eagle gold coins are limited in their appeal outside of the U.S. When the Mint was reviewing its bloated offering list in the fall of 2008 it may have wanted to keep the fractional gold Buffaloes and not the fractional gold Eagles, but the wording of the two series enabling legislation probably left it little choice. (See the enabling legislation section in Appendix C.) The Mint has indicated that it intends to continue with the $50 mint state business strike Buffalo issues without mintmarks and $50 proofs.

$50 Mint State Buffalo

Look at the total population of the $50 Buffalo gold in mint state form. The 2008-W is a tight bottleneck in the midst of a 870,000 and growing mint state population. It's the rarest one ounce gold issue since 1933 and it's ***dramatically*** rarer than the next closest sibling. Equally important is the fact that ***the Mint indicates it does not intend to make anymore "W" mintmarked gold Buffaloes so there is almost no chance of a new key coming in to compete with it in the $50 mint state set.*** The Mint by law is required to strike .999 fine $50 mint state gold every year in reasonable volume as determined by the Secretary of the Treasury.

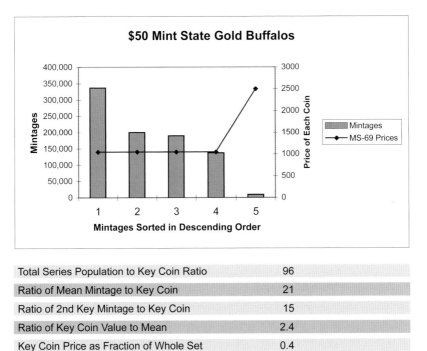

Total Series Population to Key Coin Ratio	96
Ratio of Mean Mintage to Key Coin	21
Ratio of 2nd Key Mintage to Key Coin	15
Ratio of Key Coin Value to Mean	2.4
Key Coin Price as Fraction of Whole Set	0.4

On top of having a high population series to drive it, the type set collectors who buy the $5, $10 and $25 mint state gold are likely to want to hold a 2008-W $50 to go with them. The probable convergence of type and series collectors on the same coin is encouraging. If the Mint keeps producing high volume mint state $50 Buffaloes for the next few years, the price of the 2008-W could see a MS-69 market price of $5,000.

The $50 Proof Buffalo

While the "W" $50 coins may be gone the $50 proofs are going to survive according to the Mint. So that brings us to the question, is the 2008 proof Buffalo going to endure as the $50 proof key? We know that new series have a tendency to display what the Mint calls an inaugural sales spike in year one and then see a continuous random walk deterioration until a bottom is reached sometime after the fourth year. We do know that the 2008 $50 proof's status as king is highly uncertain until the series closes. Buffalo proof type set collectors are likely to want a 2008 $50 to go with the other three 2008 fractionals, so again we can expect some collector base convergence on this coin also.

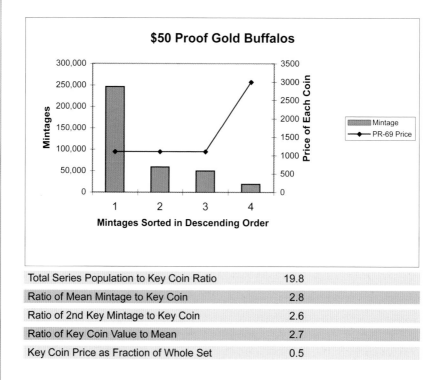

Total Series Population to Key Coin Ratio	19.8
Ratio of Mean Mintage to Key Coin	2.8
Ratio of 2nd Key Mintage to Key Coin	2.6
Ratio of Key Coin Value to Mean	2.7
Key Coin Price as Fraction of Whole Set	0.5

$25 Mint State Buffalo

In its year of issue the $25 mint state Buffalo was sold as a four coin set, a single issue and a two coin "prosperity set." Unfortunately that bumped the gold half's mintage about 8,000 coins and made it the most common 2008 fractional Buffalo issue other than the tiny $5 coins. The coin isn't date rare, it does not have a denominational set to drive it at this point, and it's type common in its set.

$25 Proof Buffalo

Proofs almost always sell better than the mint state coins because they are more attractive and they tend to pick up collector base quickly after sell out if the numbers are low enough and the design is good. If the 2008 proof Buffalo half does in fact prove to be a one year type coin its likely to be a hard to find item in the out years.

$10 Mint State Buffalo

With its 9,949 mintage and single year type coin status this coin should perform well. Even if a mint state bullion buffalo quarter comes out at some point its not likely given typical bullion production runs that the 2008W's status as denominational key would be in jeopardy.

$10 Proof Buffalo

This coin like its $25 proof sibling has a bright future if the mint does not start up fractional proof buffalo production again.

$5 Proof Buffalo and $5 Mint State Buffalo

These coins like their larger sibling have a bright future if the mint does not start up fractional buffalo production again.

This is the Mint's post regarding the elimination of most of these coins from mid 2009:

"As a result of the numismatic product portfolio analysis conducted last fall, beginning in 2009, American Buffalo Gold Proof fractional coins and the four-coin set are no longer available. Additionally, the United States Mint will no longer offer American Buffalo Gold Uncirculated Coins."

"Uncirculated coins" are the "W" mintmarked mint state finish gold Buffaloes.

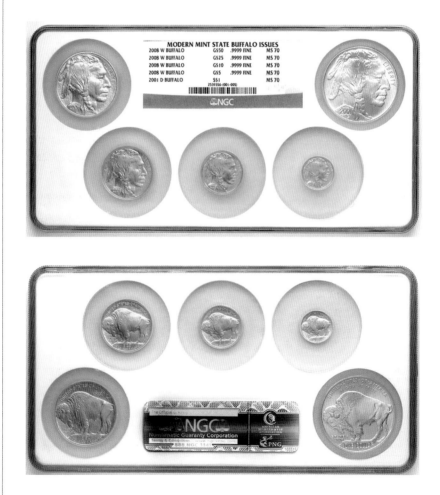

$10 Gold Eagle Commemoratives

	Mintage	69 Price
1984-W Los Angeles Olympiad Mint State Gold	75,886	$550
1984-P Los Angeles Olympiad Proof Gold	33,309	$550
1984-D Los Angeles Olympiad Proof Gold	34,533	$550
1984-S Los Angeles Olympiad Proof Gold	48,551	$550
1984-W Los Angeles Olympiad Proof Gold	381,085	$550
2000-W Library of Congress Mint State Bimetallic	6,683	$4,000
2000-W Library of Congress Proof Bimetallic	27,167	$1,000
2003–P First Flight Mint State Gold	10,129	$600
2003-P First Flight Proof Gold	21,846	$600

Mint State

The lead coin of this extremely short set is the 2000-W mint state bimetallic. Its population is almost identical to the 1915 Panama Pacific $2.5 gold commemorative's 6,749 mintage and its price looks a lot like the small Pan Pac's $3,600 typical mint state price after almost 100 years of growth! We can't attribute the bimetallic's accelerated development to large set-driven key date behavior. The mint state bimetallic picked up 100 years worth of development in 10 years because it has been promoted by strong marketers as a result of its unique characteristics. The lead coin in this set may not be over priced long-term, but the days of white-hot appreciation on a percentage basis are over.

Proof

It's interesting to see the proof bimetallic trade for over twice the price of the 20 percent rarer Wright Brothers sibling. Coins without unifying design elements really are stand-alone coins from a pricing perspective and having so few denominational set members separated by so many years magnifies this tendency. The $10 proof gold commemoratives need more members and a convincing low mintage key to help develop the collector base.

First Spouse $10 Gold

MODERN COMMEMORATIVE COINS

First Spouse $10 Gold

Year	Proof Mintages	PR-69 Prices	Mint State Mintages	MS-69 Prices
2007 Washington	20,000	$550	20,000	$550
2007 Adams	20,000	$550	20,000	$550
2007 Jefferson's Liberty	20,000	$550	20,000	$550
2007 Madison	18,300	$550	12,500	$550
2008 Monroe	7,900	$600	4,500	$600
2008 Adams	7,400	$600	4,200	$700
2008 Jackson's Liberty	7,800	$700	4,700	$750
2008 Van Buren's Liberty	7,500	$700	4,300	$775

PROJECTED SERIES MEMBERS =39+

This series has just gone through its inaugural spike and has seen its sales rates collapse in dramatic fashion. The Mint has indicated its intention to reduce the number of its offerings, increase inventory turn over and stay clear of coins that don't sell in excess of 10,000 units a year but their "hands are tied" by Congress on this series. They are forced to finish it out no matter how poorly it sells and that could make this set interesting. If the Mint makes good on its statement that fractional changing reverse platinum eagles, and low mintage mint marked gold are a thing of the past this series could be the only issue available directly from the U.S. government with sub 6,000 mintages going forward. The considerations that will influence the long-term behavior of this set are many.

LIBERTY SUB SERIES: The Presidents who were not married during their terms in office have classic coinage designs used instead of wives. This has created a subset that enjoys some semblance of broad acceptance and consistently attractive designs. The commensurate bump in potential demand in this subset is helpful but the higher initial mintages that come with it are not. Sub 5,000 mintage Liberty issues have favorable fundamentals. The Jefferson, Jackson, Van Buren and Buchanan Liberty members are pictured on page 160.

MELTING: The first three issues combined saw roughly 10,000 pieces melted by the large bullion houses in 2007-2008. Unlike gold Eagles that are a widely recognized and traded standard that sell for a few percent over melt for common mint state dates, these coins are purchased as junk bullion and melted into standard bars. This practice makes the mintage charts unreliable.

EXPENSIVE: This series is a very long set of coins that cost over $600 each from the Mint.

The complete set is likely to cost over $25,000 and the expense is going to encourage collectors to cherry pick the designs they like and pass over the ones they don't.

DESIGN COHESION: This set lacks a stable design element. An "Unstable Design Model" as described in Chapter 4 is likely.

These are the series' relative rarity price curves for the proof and mint state coins respectively.

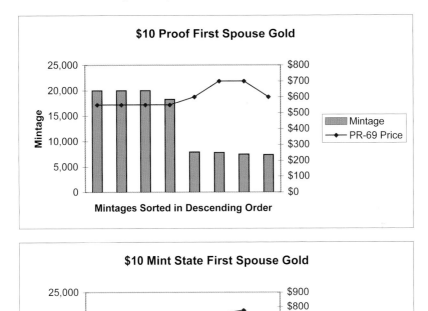

Notice that the mint state Jackson and Van Buren issues with their roughly 4,700 and 4,300 mintages are already stronger than their slightly rarer and older generic siblings.

In order for the generic issues of the series to overcome the advantages possessed by the Liberty short set they will likely need more than a marginal mintage advantage. Either a Liberty issue or yet to be revealed sub 4,000 mintage generic is likely to end up dominant.

If a sub 4,000 mintage issue does in fact materialize in 2010 as is likely based on sales report behavior available as of the end of 2009, we can expect an after market price response to the anomaly. A lift in succeeding issue demand may produce a situation where these coins go from consistently selling well short of the number of coins struck to a series of successive sellouts.

The Mint "strikes to anticipated demand" and the numbers that they have to look at from 2009 through the first half of 2010 are going to be in the 3,000-5,000 range for mint state spouses and 6,000-8,000 range for proofs. The point is the final number of these coins in the hands of the public is not just dependent on public demand. It's dependent on how many coins the Mint "anticipates" will be needed and right now they don't see any demand.

The Hawaiian half is not great just because its low mintage. Its outstanding because the reverse design is iconic *and* its low mintage. Some of these coins are beautiful and either through momentary absence of demand or Mint anticipation of poor demand are likely to have the combination of looks and rarity needed to become note worthy eventually.

$20 Ultra High Relief Gold Eagle

	Mintage	MS-69 Price
2009 Ultra High Relief $20 Gold Eagle	100,000+	$1,500

The 2009 Ultra High Relief $20 gold Eagle is the ultimate expression of Augustus Saint-Gaudens' original design concept and it was received by the collecting community with great anticipation. The excitement did not translate into runaway sales numbers due to the planchet shortage present at the time, the almost constant month or more shipment delay, a very poor economy suppressing demand plus the one coin per customer limit that was imposed through late July 2009.

This coin is not a sub 6,000 mintage modern design based rarity possessing a slot in the top fifty type coin ranking but that's not necessary for a coin with this kind of market draw. It is the ultimate expression of the 1986-present modern gold eagles just as the 1907 high relief gold is the ultimate type coin of the 1907-1933 set. There are plenty of old saints with lower combined NGC and PCGS populations than the 1907 high relief's roughly 5,000 surviving population, but they don't bring anything like the typical 1907 high relief's $10,000-$40,000 price tag. We can expect to see the same behavior to show up over time with the 2009 Ultra High Relief but to a much lesser degree because there are so many more of them.

Platinum Eagles:
The Rarest Type Set Since World War I

MODERN COMMEMORATIVE COINS

Proof Platinum Eagles

Who would have thought that we would see a type set with a mint-age table that looks like this in our lifetime? *This set holds 16 of the 50 rarest proof type coins in production since 1859.* U.S. collectors have not been afforded the opportunity to collect such rare proof design-based type coins in set form since the four-coin matte proof Indian and Saint-Gaudens gold faded from the scene in 1915.

Proof Platinum Eagle Mintages

YEAR	$100	$50	$25	$10
1997 Proof-Eagle Over Sun	20,851	15,431	18,628	36,993
1998 Proof-New England	14,912	13,836	14,873	19,847
1999 Proof-Wet Lands	12,363	11,103	13,507	19,133
2000 Proof-Heart Land	12,453	11,049	11,995	15,651
2001 Proof-South West	8,969	8,254	8,847	12,174
2002 Proof-North West	9,834	8,772	9,282	12,365
2003 Proof-Patriotic Vigilance	8,246	7,131	7,044	9,534
2004 Proof-Seated America	6,007	5,063	5,193	7,161
2005 Proof-Plenty	6,602	5,942	6,592	8,104
2006 Proof-Legislative	9,152	7,649	7,813	10,205
2007 Proof-Executive	8,363	22,873	6,017	8,176
2007 Reverse Proof-Executive	-	16,937	-	-
2008 Proof-Judicial	4,769	4,020	4,153	5,138
2009 Proof-Perfect Union	*8,000	-	-	-

The proof platinum Eagles were the very first set to enjoy the Mint's new changing reverse collector series structure. This is the set that paved the way conceptually for all the common changing reverse series that have come after it. *The set's consistent Statue of Liberty obverse gives the proof platinum Eagles outstanding series cohesion that produces the very desirable relative rarity pricing structure. The changing reverses protect the very low mintage keys from ever becoming just a high population type coin.*

In addition to being rare, cohesive and design differentiated, *the set enjoys the benefit of consistently excellent reverse designs because the Mint had a completely free hand in selecting the themes and artwork without the interference of special interest groups.*

Starting in 1998, a five-year "Vistas of Liberty" set showing a bald eagle flying over various parts of our great country was produced. It was followed by a coin struck in 2003 called "Patriotic Vigilance,"

"Vistas of Liberty" set
(1998-2002)

whose design was developed soon after the attack on 9-11. The theme "America the Land of Plenty " inspired Elizabeth Jones to develop a reverse based on Daniel Chester French's Statute of America seated outside the New York Customs House for 2004. Precious little design work was done for 2005, so one of the runner-up designs from the previous year showing an eagle perched on a cornucopia was pressed into service. Then came what is likely to prove to be one of the greatest of all modern subsets, the three-coin "Foundations of American Democracy" set representing our three branches of government for 2006, 2007 and 2008. *All type coins in mint state or proof finish with mintages less than 4,200 coins since 1915 are in the "Foundations" themed subset* as of this writing.

2004

2005

"Foundations of American Democracy" set (2006-2008)

As we covered earlier, we want as many troubled infancy issues as possible to converge on the keys of our chosen series to promote the rarity necessary for greatness without making the set impossible to complete or compromise its beauty.

Platinum's Troubled Infancy Issues

TOO EXPENSIVE: The platinum Eagles since their year of issue have consistently been the most expensive issue offered by the United States Mint and sales volumes have suffered.

SHORT SALES PERIODS: These coins are almost always among the last coins each year to be offered for sale.

DILUTION OF COLLECTOR DEMAND: The "W" mint state platinum Eagles with changing reverses split the platinum collector base in 2006, 2007 and 2008.

SELLING FOR MELT: Large denomination "common date" platinum eagles were sold off to bullion houses in mass when platinum's price spiked to over $2,000 an ounce. Exactly what their fate has been or will be is uncertain but there is no question that a least some have seen hardship and will not be returning to the collectors hands in the condition they once were if at all.

MATERIAL RISK: The Mint normally strikes the changing reverse platinum Eagles in the spring and in 2008 that meant buying planchet material at a cost of about $2,000 an ounce. The Mint spent well over $30 million to produce a little over 30,000 coins whose quality were good enough to sell in their proof and "W" programs. Apparently the

Mints personnel correctly surmised that down side material risk was dramatic and short struck the horrendously expensive four-coin sets to partially compensate. True to form shortly after the initial sales rush the price of platinum crashed forcing a lengthy suspension of sales and eventual repricing at a little more than half the initial offering price. *The Mint lost millions.*

After diluting the collector base with too many silver, gold and platinum issues and suffering staggering losses on the platinum Eagles, the *Mint announced toward the end of 2008 that no more proof platinum Eagle fractionals would be produced for the foreseeable future.* Given that the Mint is required by law to make a profit on its offerings and given the extreme volatility associated with platinum, it is unlikely that future administrations will reinstate them.

This is a very helpful development if it holds true. Series currently in production are constantly under threat of having their existing key date overtaken by a succeeding year. This adds an element of risk in buying immature keys at aftermarket prices prior to series closure. *Collectors of the fractional proof platinum Eagles thankfully can go find something else to worry about ... like completing their chosen denominational set of the rarest proof type coins issued in almost half our country's coinage history before the pathetically small populations find permanent homes.*

The fractional platinum Eagles are also blessed to have the right number of members in each denominations set. Twelve proof coins are enough to give the sets breadth but not so numerous that putting together a set of high material content coins becomes a burden. *The potential generated by having 11 of the strongest type coins in the last 100 years or so rolling down behind an extraordinarily strong and lovely infant key is hard to overstate.*

$10 Proof Platinum Eagles 1997 to 2008

$10 Proof Platinum Eagles	Mintage	Price
1997 Proof-Eagle Over Sun	36,993	$150
1998 Proof-New England	19,847	$150
1999 Proof-Wet Lands	19,133	$150
2000 Proof-Heart Land	15,651	$150
2001 Proof-South West	12,174	$170
2002 Proof-North West	12,365	$160
2003 Proof-Patriotic Vigilance	9,534	$235
2004 Proof-Seated America	7,161	$600
2005 Proof-Plenty	8,104	$225
2006 Proof-Legislative	10,205	$175
2007 Proof-Executive	8,176	$200
2008 Proof-Judicial	5,138	$400

12 Coin PR-69 Set Cost=		**$2,700**
Melt at $1,250 Platinum =	**$1,500**	

$1 Gold Commemoratives	Mintage	Price
1903 Louisiana Pur./ Jefferson	17,500	$900
1903 Louisiana Pur./ McKinley	17,500	$800
1904-05 Lewis and Clark	20,066	$1,500
1915-S Panama Pacific	15,000	$700
1916-17 McKinley Memorial	19,977	$600
1922 Grant Memorial-Both	10,016	$2,000

6 Coin MS-63 Type Set Cost=		**$6,500**
Melt at $1,000 Gold=	**$300**	

In order to get back down to design based series of similar physical size and rarity class we need to go back to the $1 gold commemoratives of the 1903 to 1922 period.

For a relatively inexpensive classic gold type set the $1 gold commemoratives posses impressive design based rarity because the period of production for each design was only one or two years. A complete design-based six-coin $1 set in typical MS-63 grade cost over $6,000 to complete. *The $10 proof platinum Eagles compare favorably in that they are each their own type coin and eleven out of the twelve rank among the rarest 100 proof type coins issued since 1859.* The $10 proof platinum Eagles in general have much rarer design based keys than the $1 gold commemoratives and they can be purchased for less than $3,000.

If we look back at the section on interdenominational value growth we found that David has the tendency to slay Goliath on a percentage basis. There is little doubt that this set will show greater collector base growth over the next 10 years than any of its larger siblings because its so affordable. As is obvious the $10 proof platinum Eagle set is one of the cheapest precious metal complete sets in all of American numismatics but it's struck on $1,500 worth of material that's over 10 times rarer than gold. When platinum spiked to $2,300 an ounce recently, platinum collectors on the PCGS message boards and other informal networks found that almost no one turned in $10 proof platinum Eagles to be sold for melt. What this means is the mintage chart that you see is still an accurate guide to the relatively rarity of the series members and the semi keys are not going to have much chance of becoming rarer than the keys as a result of melting or mishandling during periods of very high precious metals prices.

Once again, the relative rarity price profile shows a badly under priced key date going through the typical market inventory absorption period.

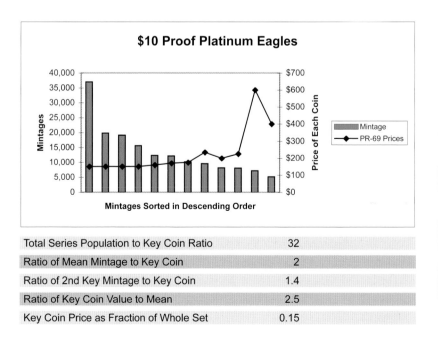

Total Series Population to Key Coin Ratio	32
Ratio of Mean Mintage to Key Coin	2
Ratio of 2nd Key Mintage to Key Coin	1.4
Ratio of Key Coin Value to Mean	2.5
Key Coin Price as Fraction of Whole Set	0.15

$25 Proof Platinum Eagles 1997 to 2008

$25 Proof Platinum Eagles	Mintage	69-Price
1997 Proof-Eagle Over Sun	18,628	$400
1998 Proof-New England	14,873	$400
1999 Proof-Wet Lands	13,507	$400
2000 Proof-Heart Land	11,995	$400
2001 Proof-South West	8,847	$400
2002 Proof-North West	9,282	$400
2003 Proof-Patriotic Vigilance	7,044	$425
2004 Proof-Seated America	5,193	$1,100
2005 Proof-Plenty	6,592	$500
2006 Proof-Legislative	7,813	$400
2007 Proof-Executive	6,017	$500
2008 Proof-Judicial	4,153	$700

Total 12 Coin Set Price		**$6,000**
Melt Value @ $1,250 Platinum	$3,750	
Average Mintage 4 Rarest	5,488	

$5 MS Gold Commemoratives	Mintage	69 Price
2006 San Francisco $5 Gold	16,230	$350
1995 Torch Runner $5 Gold	14,675	$850
2008 Bald Eagle $5 Gold	13,467	$350
1995 Civil War $5 Gold	12,735	$900
1997 Roosevelt $5 Gold	11,894	$1,500
2002 Salt Lake City $5 Gold	10,585	$400
1995 Stadium $5 Gold	10,579	$2,000
1996 Cauldron $5 Gold	9,210	$2,000
1996 Flag Bearer $5 Gold	9,174	$2,000
1996 Smithsonian $5 Gold	9,068	$850
2001 Capital V. Center $5 Gold	6,761	$1,600
1997 Jackie Robinson $5 Gold	5,174	$4,000

Total Cost of 12 Lead Coins		**$16,800**
Melt Value @ $1,000 Gold	$2,700	
Average Mintage 4 Rarest	7,544	

**Half of the $25 proof platinum Eagles rank among the top 50 rarest design-based proof type coins issued by the Federal government since 1859 and all of them are in the top 100.** The chart on the next page illustrates clearly that the keys to this set are undervalued because they are young and have not had time to work through the typical 10-year maturation and dealer inventory dissipation process

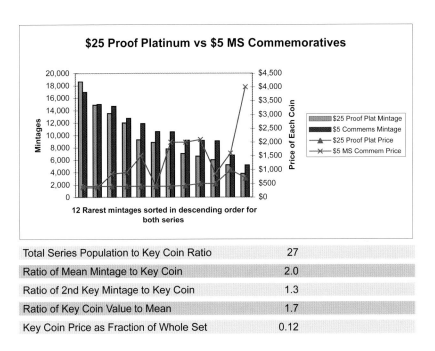

$25 Proof Platinum vs $5 MS Commemoratives

12 Rarest mintages sorted in descending order for both series

Legend:
- $25 Proof Plat Mintage
- $5 Commems Mintage
- $25 Proof Plat Price
- $5 MS Commem Price

Total Series Population to Key Coin Ratio	27
Ratio of Mean Mintage to Key Coin	2.0
Ratio of 2nd Key Mintage to Key Coin	1.3
Ratio of Key Coin Value to Mean	1.7
Key Coin Price as Fraction of Whole Set	0.12

The $25 cameo proof platinum Eagles are a lovely set whose lead coins are the second and sixth rarest proof type coins issued since World War I to the general public. The seated America proof from 2004 has the same 5,000 coin mintage as the uncirculated Jackie Robinson $5 gold but trades at one-fourth the price. The 2008 $25 judicial Eagles' tiny 4,153 population just needs some time to find homes so its price can stretch out from the common dates. The bottom line is the $25 proof platinum Eagle sets members are rarer than the 12 leading coins in the $5 mint state gold commemorative series, has greater material content to back their purchase price and for the moment are dramatically less expensive to acquire. Like their $10 proof siblings, the proof platinum quarters by and large were not sold off for melt even at $2,300 platinum, according to the large bullion houses and dealers surveyed at the time. The mintage chart will stay dependable and its keys will do well unless the price of platinum becomes really obscene.

The $25 proof platinum Eagle sets combination of astounding type rarity, affordability and resistance to potential developmental pitfalls makes it one of if not the finest full set collecting opportunity covered in this text.

$50 Proof Platinum Eagles 1997 to 2008

$50 Proof Platinum Eagles	Mintage	69-Price
1997 Proof-Eagle Over Sun	15,431	$800
1998 Proof-New England	13,836	$800
1999 Proof-Wet Lands	11,103	$800
2000 Proof-Heart Land	11,049	$800
2001Proof-South West	8,254	$800
2002 Proof-North West	8,772	$800
2003 Proof-Patriotic Vigilance	7,131	$850
2004 Proof-Seated America	5,063	$1,600
2005 Proof-Plenty	5,942	$950
2006 Proof-Legislative	7,649	$825
2007 Proof-Executive	22,873	$750
2007 Reverse Proof-Executive	16,937	$800
2008 Proof-Judicial	4,020	$1,400
Total 13 Coin Proof Set		**$12,000**
Melt Value @ $1,250 Platinum	**$8,125**	
Average Mintage 4 Rarest	**5,539**	

Proof Walking Liberty Halves	Mintage	65 Price
1936 Proof Half	3,901	$4,500
1937 Proof Half	5,728	$1,200
1938 Proof Half	8,152	$950
1939 Proof Half	8,808	$800
1940 Proof Half	11,279	$700
1941 Proof Half	15,412	$700
1942 Proof Half	21,120	$700
Total 7 Coin Proof Set		**$9,550**
Melt Value @ $15 Silver	**$40**	
Average Mintage 4 Rarest	**6,647**	

Five of the proof platinum Eagle halves are among the 50 rarest proof design-based type coins issued since 1859. The 2008 Judicial half is the rarest proof type coin issued to the public since the great gold matte proofs faded from the scene almost 100 years ago. The semi key to this set, the 2004 Seated America half, is the fourth rarest proof type coin issued to the general public since 1915 and it did not come in a mint state form.

When a series is issued in both proof and mint state form on a routine basis and for some reason the Mint suspends production of the mint state issues it has a tendency to force the collector bases of the mint state and proof series to cross thus creating stronger pricing than would normally be expected for the rarity class. The 2004 and 2005 proof platinum halves with their 5,063 and 5,942 mintages are so rare to start with that if a cross series bump shows up they could be very strong semi keys. The reverse designs in 1997, 2006, 2007 and 2008 were offered in both mint state and proof form.

The Mint selected the halves to be the 10th anniversary set in order to keep the price reasonable and still have coins large enough to be impressive. Many collectors may select this set as their first choice for the same reason. Unfortunately, for those who bought the platinum 10th anniversary set, the Mint struck 30,000 of them and sold them in 2007 and 2008. Even with lovely packaging and an extended sales period the Mint could not sell 30,000 sets but they did manage to sell about 17,000. There are two benefits of this: First, the total population of the $50 set's common dates jumped by almost 40 percent in one year and common dates are silent advertisements for the keys. Second, some silver and gold anniversary set collectors will have a tendency to want all anniversary set forms and their two-coin running start on the platinum halves may encourage them to continue with it.

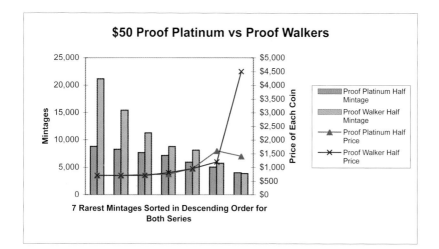

Total Series Population to Key Coin Ratio	34
Ratio of Mean Mintage to Key Coin	2.2
Ratio of 2nd Key Mintage to Key Coin	1.3
Ratio of Key Coin Value to Mean	1.8
Key Coin Price as Fraction of Whole Set	0.12

The proof Walking Liberty halves are the only decent reference point we have to help us deduce the $50 proof platinum Eagles' potential. Notice the 2004 platinum Eagle is under valued. Long-term it's unlikely to trade for the same price as the 1937 Walker. The Seated America proof has about 100 times the intrinsic value of a Walking Liberty half. It has a 5,063 mintage as opposed to 5,728 and ranks about 33rd in terms of proof type rarity since 1859, while the 1937 Walker comes in at 127th. It is highly likely that the 2004 proof half will trade well over $2,500 in inflation-adjusted dollars at maturity for a mid-grade coin.

The 2008 proof platinum half is likely to rival or surpass the 1936 Walker at maturity. It possesses similar date and mintmark rarity, dramatically superior design-based rarity, about 100 times the intrinsic value and has a larger, more populous set to drive it. The judicial $50 Eagle has nothing to fear from the prospect of endless design proliferation one day producing a design-based collecting culture.

The only real problem with the $50 set is if the price of platinum spikes over $2,000 an ounce and stays there. The $50 proof platinum Eagle key date's price could suffer and the mintage tables could become inaccurate through the process described in the section on page 74 titled "Common Dates Sold for Melt."

Cameo proof platinum eagle sets are pictured at right and they bear a haunting similarity to the very popular commemorative quarter and dollar sets. There is no question that platinum Eagles are the high-end expression of this revolutionary structure.

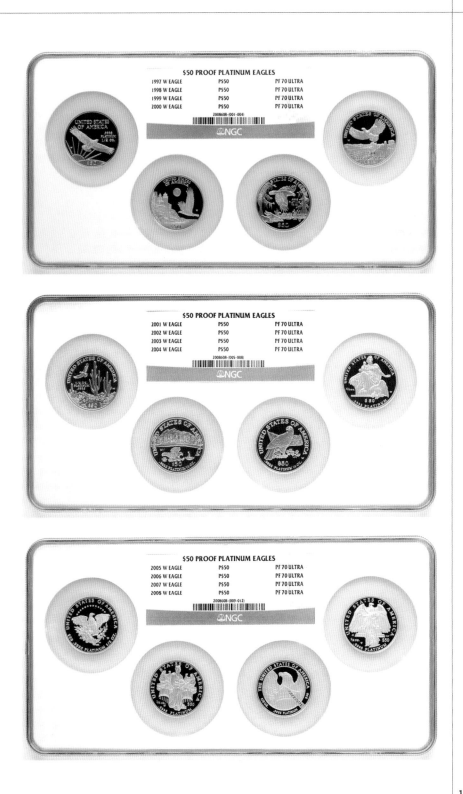

$50 PROOF PLATINUM EAGLES

1997 W EAGLE	PS50	PF 70 ULTRA
1998 W EAGLE	PS50	PF 70 ULTRA
1999 W EAGLE	PS50	PF 70 ULTRA
2000 W EAGLE	PS50	PF 70 ULTRA

2008608-(001-004)

NGC

$50 PROOF PLATINUM EAGLES

2001 W EAGLE	PS50	PF 70 ULTRA
2002 W EAGLE	PS50	PF 70 ULTRA
2003 W EAGLE	PS50	PF 70 ULTRA
2004 W EAGLE	PS50	PF 70 ULTRA

2008608-(005-008)

NGC

$50 PROOF PLATINUM EAGLES

2005 W EAGLE	PS50	PF 70 ULTRA
2006 W EAGLE	PS50	PF 70 ULTRA
2007 W EAGLE	PS50	PF 70 ULTRA
2008 W EAGLE	PS50	PF 70 ULTRA

2008608-(009-012)

NGC

$100 Proof Platinum Eagles

	Mintage	69 Price
1997 Proof-Eagle Over Sun	20,851	$1,700
1998 Proof-New England	14,912	$1,600
1999 Proof-Wet Lands	12,363	$1,600
2000 Proof-Heart Land	12,453	$1,600
2001 Proof-South West	8,969	$1,600
2002 Proof-North West	9,834	$1,600
2003 Proof-Patriotic Vigilance	8,246	$1,800
2004 Proof-Seated America	6,007	$2,400
2005 Proof-Plenty	6,602	$1,800
2006 Proof-Legislative	9,152	$1,600
2007 Proof-Executive	9,268	$1,600
2008 Proof-Judicial	4,769	$2,200
2009 Proof- Perfect Union	*8,000	$1,700
TOTAL POPULATION	**131,000**	

According to the U.S. Mint, this is the only proof platinum denomination that will continue and its new reverse theme will be a multi-year run celebrating the Preamble to the Constitution. The elimination of the other denominations is expected to force a partial convergence of the platinum Eagle collector bases. The $100 Eagle collectors will likely continue to purchase their set requirements. Four-coin set buyers can certainly afford to pick up a $100 issue every year and some of the fractional collectors wishing to hold one of every design will make the transition if they can afford it.

The bottom line is demand will be more concentrated. The Mint's decision to limit the $100 Perfect Union coin to a mintage of 8,000

coins with a household limit of five coins is interesting. Obviously, if they are placing household limits on the coins the Mint's marketing department thinks there is more than enough demand to pull the 8,000 coins offered the public. If that's the case, limited planchets and time in late 2009 may be part of the reason the limit was set at 8,000 as opposed to some other higher number. *One of the important points we can take away from these changes is that the 2008 Judicial issue is likely to be the key for a while.*

The wealthy collectors tend to seek what they view as the best material and frequently that means the larger denominations. This coin is the largest denomination ever struck and offered to the public by the Federal government. Assuming the six-coin "Preamble" sub series goes to completion and precious metal values remain stable, a complete PR-69 set will cost well over $30,000 and that's if the 2008 key and the 2004 semi key don't move into the $5,000 and $3,000 price range, respectively. This set is not for the faint of heart or wallet.

Another issue that will mold this set and its collector base over the years will be the price of platinum. As is obvious from the chart below, the price of the common dates is dictated by the intrinsic value of platinum. When the material price spiked in early 2008, $100 coins were sold off in droves to bullion houses like Kitco and SilverTowne. The price of the then key 2004 proof stayed flat as the price of platinum sky-rocketed and then crashed from $3,000 to about $1,800 when material prices dropped because so may sets were scrapped to be sold for their bullion content. When Kitco and SilverTowne employees questioned as to the fate of these coins they made it clear that the melting point of platinum is so great it was not worth the trouble to melt platinum Eagles. One Kitco employee said, "We deal in circulated bullion, we don't go out of our way to protect (special issues) or harm them." Many of these coins went to non-numismatic homes and some will not return to the coin market in the condition they left it.

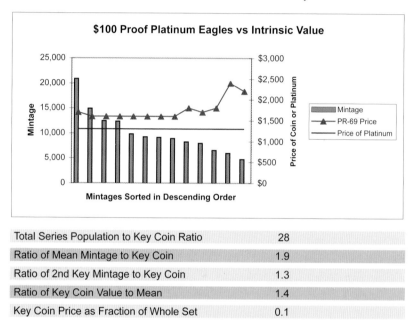

$100 Proof Platinum Eagles vs Intrinsic Value

Total Series Population to Key Coin Ratio	28
Ratio of Mean Mintage to Key Coin	1.9
Ratio of 2nd Key Mintage to Key Coin	1.3
Ratio of Key Coin Value to Mean	1.4
Key Coin Price as Fraction of Whole Set	0.1

The 1927-D Saint-Gaudens double eagle is not rare because it was low mintage. There were 12 double eagles with lower mintage figures. The government destroyed them because the official price of gold almost doubled in 1933. Platinum is more than 10 times rarer than gold and in many ways much more useful. Wide price swings can be expected. Even if the coins aren't melted it may be hard to determine how many of each design will survive in an attractive form.

This series may in the end prove to be the King of Kings among coinage issued since the Great Depression, but its path to greatness may be turbulent and the values of its keys may get battered from time to time. If they do in fact become mega coins it may be a result of the so called "common dates" with sub 9,000 mintages going "under water" and being sold for melt one too many times.

Changing Reverse Mint State Platinum Eagles

YEAR	$100	$50	$25	$10
2006-W Mint State Legislative	3,068	2,577	2,676	3,544
2007-W Mint State Executive	4,177	3,635	3,690	5,556
2008-W Mint State Judicial	2,876	2,253	2,481	3,706

There are only a handful of mint state type coins made available to the collecting public since 1915 with sub 4,000 mintages and all 10 of them are members of the 12-coin Foundations of American Democracy platinum Eagle subset. The question is, a subset of what? Are they going to be collected as part of the business strike platinum bullion date based series or as a rider on the changing reverse proof platinum Eagles? Will they be collected as their own exclusive set? Time will answer these questions but one thing is certain. They are the pinnacle of modern type rarity and they are the lead coins in the complete platinum Eagle type set. The $50 platinum Eagle denominational type set is listed below as an example.

That's an awful lot of design variety and type in some form will dominate how the platinum set is assembled. The existing collector base is populated primarily by the cameo proof collectors because the cameos are so lovely and have had time to develop a following. But when proof collectors finish their sets, will they want to go on and pick up the ultra low mintage three-coin Foundations of American Democracy mint state issues? Would you?

The cameo proofs are clearly a date run type set, but will the mint state coins also be collected in the same manner? A complete mint state set composed of all four designs can only be put together as a date run using the 2005, 2006, 2007 and 2008 issues because 2009 mint state platinum Eagles were not struck in any form. The 2005 platinum Eagles are the second or third rarest business strike platinum Eagle in every denomination and they were issued in bulk so the majority of them are imperfect and have no chance of grading MS-70, while most of the 2006-2008 issues can. MS-70 2005 platinum Eagles may perform better than their population reports would indicate due to preferential absorption. ***On the next page is an example of a complete mint state date run of all four reverse designs in a PCGS multi coin holder. The set shown is the rarest mint state type set since the five-coin Panama Pacific Commemorative issues came out prior to World War I.***

While the 200-year mint state design based rarity ranking shown on page 57 is an imperfect approximation, it's noteworthy that the $50 mint state platinum eagles shown come in 18th, 27th, 38th and 179th with mintages of 2,253, 2,577, 3,635 and 52,852, respectively. Regardless of which denomination you chose to look at these changing reverse mint state populations are so low that a relatively small influx of new collectors willing to see the favorable fundamentals can absorb the keys. ***There are very few places at this table.***

The Eagle over the Sun reverse platinum Eagles are not included in the design based rarity rankings because as of this writing there is no way to know final total populations until the end of the program is announced.

Mint State Platinum Eagles-Business Strikes

	$100	$50	$25	$10
1997-2003 Issues Struck as Reverse Proofs				
1997	56,000	20,500	27,100	70,250
1998	133,002	32,419	38,887	39,525
1999	56,707	32,309	39,734	55,955
2000	10,003	18,892	20,054	34,027
2001	14,070	12,815	21,815	52,017
2002	11,502	24,005	27,405	23,005
2003	8,007	17,409	25,207	22,007
TOTALS	**289,291**	**158,349**	**200,202**	**296,786**
2004-2008 Issues Struck as Plain Mint State Finish				
2004	7,009	13,236	18,010	15,010
2005	6,310	9,013	12,013	14,013
2006	6,000	9,602	12,001	11,001
2007	7,202	7,001	8,402	13,003
2008	21,800	14,000	22,800	17,000
CURRENT TOTALS	**48,321**	**52,852**	**73,226**	**70,027**

When this program was initiated in 1997 the Mint wanted the platinum Eagles to be special so they gave them high denominations, struck the proofs with changing reverses and the standard business issues with reverse proof surfaces. The reverse proofs are attractive and look a lot like the silver, gold and platinum anniversary issues of 2006 and 2007. Unfortunately, the very low margins on the early platinum Eagles struck for sale to the bullion dealer network could not justify the time and cost associated with hand polishing the dies, so the practice was suspended in 2004. The recent issues have a traditional mint state finish.

All the issues in all four denominations at this point trade for bullion value plus a small fraction in MS-69 and that certainly puts a nice floor under the set's purchase price at this time. The four denominations on the surface look like they have potential. The $10 and $25 issues have low mintages compared to their price and while their total populations are not massive they certainly look like they are capable of putting pressure on the lowest mintage issues at some point. The same can be said for the large coins to a lesser degree.

Below is a composite mintage profile of this set assuming you don't count the changing reverse mint state Foundations of American Democracy as members.

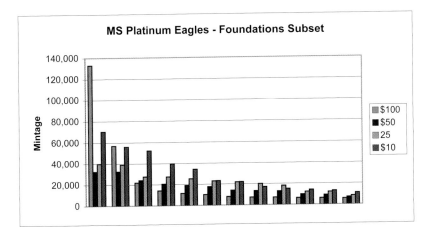

The profile is typical with what looks like shallow keys ... until we add in the Foundations subset.

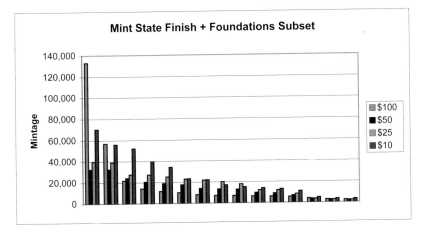

The stable reverse coins as an exclusive set have zero type rarity and shallow relatively high mintage keys. When you assume that the standard reverse coins will face direct competition from the changing reverse platinum eagles the situation becomes dramatically worse. As was clearly demonstrated in the section "Unstable Design Models" and "Ramifications of Merging Stable and Unstable Series" date rare series that have to compete for collectors in a design rich structure fair very poorly unless their populations are truly massive and their keys posses profound rarity that eclipses that of the changing reverse sub set. But this is not the case. The Foundations changing reverse subset is dramatically rarer than the stable issues and that's a formula for disaster in common mint state grades.

2007 American Eagle
Platinum Reverse Proof

CHAPTER 11

A PERFECT STORM OF OPPORTUNITY

We have entered a very exciting period of opportunity
for coin collectors that we have not seen since the 1906 to
1936 era. New designs are pouring into the hands of the
collecting and general public at a rate that we have never
seen in our 200-plus years of coinage history. It is precisely
the convergence of the new design-based era, the dilution
of collector demand from too many competing issues, high
material prices, shortages of raw planchets in 2008 and the
subsequent unbelievably low type coin mintages appearing
just as series are being closed that has created the perfect
storm of opportunity we see today.

Numerous examples of the impact high levels of design variety can have on date and mintmark rare coins have been sighted. ***You don't want a series you collect by date and mintmark to become collected by type. Stable design series that can be completed with massive total series populations and very tight key dates are likely to pull through the design tsunami successfully.*** Despite the periodic claims that adding a changing reverse to a stable series will energize demand for the back dates, the preponderance of the long-term data seems to suggest otherwise. The only thing that gets truly energized on a percentage basis is the key dates to the new changing reverse set.

The "collector series," as the Mint likes to refer to them, ***with stable obverse and changing reverse have the most to gain from the current trends if they have enough rarity to create tight population bottlenecks.*** Constant obverse design elements enforce order and cohesion so the series behaves according to the strict and desirable discipline associated with the relative rarity models just as the classic series have over the years. The changing reverse each year protects the keys from ever becoming regarded as type common. It's insurance that's enjoyable to look at.

Another form of insurance that moderns struck on the precious metals enjoy is the value floor afforded them by their material

content. When you can buy a set of coins in which half its members rank in the top 50 rarest type coins since 1859 for less than twice melt, the risks are few and the potential rewards are many. ***Remember that collector premiums are based on the disposable income of U.S. citizens and in times of hardship the market can lose its liquidity quickly. High material content issues are liquid and low risk.*** Conversely, attractive high grade precious metal series issued prior to World War II frequently have only 2 percent of their value backed by material content.

Over half of a mature set's value is contained in the four rarest coins in the set. This is why it's so important to pick up series keys in their infancy before their values "stretch out" from the common dates. Yesterday's moderns that have become today's classics have already gone through the early exponential growth phase and unfortunately we missed it because most of us were not alive at the time. But the structures that created the great issues of the past are present again today. Modern series are the growth segment.

The seriously strong key dates reviewed in this text may no longer be a prudent purchase if they experience several hundred percent price increases in a short period of time. Remember that even very low mintage keys in popular series tend to see their values stall around $5,000. It's not true that opportunity only knocks once. She knocks and knocks and knocks at our door. This text has detailed tell-tale signs to look for in newer high potential issues that present themselves from time to time. Wait for the next train out, but get off your wallet when it shows up. Great coins are not normally cheap and they certainly will not stay that way long.

Those new to numismatics should start small and "get their education" before spending a significant percentage of their net worth on a coin collection. Coins are a very enjoyable hobby and a form of savings. Maybe even a superior form of savings due to avalanching Federal obligations, which we will touch on in Chapter 13.

If your funds are limited then it is prudent to spend your collecting dollars on multiple smaller denomination high potential issues or series, preferably those with precious metal content.

CHAPTER 12

PRIMARY RECOMMENDATIONS

Excellent collecting opportunities in any given time period normally boil down to a couple dozen key coins. The hard part is recognizing them while they are still affordable and available. Let's walk through the current and recent series and try to pinpoint the best places to look for the coins tomorrow's numismatic historians may write

Circulating

• The backflow of coinage to the Treasury created by the current economic weakness is creating abnormally low mintages that are beneficial to circulating coinage collectors. The 2009-2010 period may prove to be a unique opportunity. The 2009 annual mint sets in particular are interesting in that they carry the Life of Lincoln copper cents which are offered nowhere else, the very low mintage Territories quarters, plus five changing reverse golden dollars.

Silver

• Grab onto the 50 proof silver America the Beautiful quarters as they are issued beginning in 2010. As we have seen with the 1999 proof sets, great rarity is not needed to drive the issues because the collector base they attract in their price range is so large. One of them will have a slight dip before the series closes so you will end up with your key. Those that missed the 50 states quarters should just go catch the next train out.

Proposed designs for the America the Beautiful quarters.

• All the mint state silver Eagles with the "W" mintmarks are likely to behave in a manner similar to the Carson City Morgans. If you don't want to chase all the back date silver Eagles you may just wish to collect the "W" mintmarked subset. The structural similarity between the Morgan dollars and the silver Eagle dollars is amazing. ***They ARE the new Morgan.***

• The 1996 mint state silver dollar commemoratives issued with sub 16,000 mintages are the rarest silver dollars issued since the Great Depression. The limitation associated with these three coins is that their designs are not exceptionally beautiful and the set they lead lacks strong series cohesion. They are worthy of special mention nonetheless.

189

Gold

• The 1999-W, 2006-W, 2007-W and 2008-W $5 and $10 mint state gold Eagles all have excellent long-term fundamentals. They have very small mintages in the midst of attractive multimillion total series populations. The relative bottlenecks in these very affordable gold series is especially acute with the 1999-W keys and their 2008-W siblings. Collecting four-coin "W" mintmarked sets in both denominations is likely good policy.

If the rate at which fresh rolls of 1999-W $10 mint state gold Eagles are discovered and submitted to the grading services continues to deteriorate at its recent pace then the combined NGC and PCGS population report may only show 3,200 coins by the year 2020 and effectively stall thereafter. A flurry of resubmits in the presence of an appreciating market could skew this number, but not change the result. An example of this coin that is free of small bag marks may be almost unobtainable in 20 years.

• 2007-W, 2006-W and 2008-W mint state $25 gold Eagles have a bright future. The 2007-W has the lowest mintage in the denomination and really doesn't have any viable competitors for the status of series key thanks to the absence of a 1999-W issue.

• The 2008-W $50 mint state gold Eagles are in a deep mintage hole and if purchased at less than 1.5 times melt may be a good long-term buy.

• First Spouse $10 gold could find itself the only low mintage issue offered by the Mint for the foreseeable future. The apparent disinterest in producing anything with less than 10,000-30,000 annual sales could play into this series' hands. Congress has required that this denominational set go on to completion regardless of how few sell. Liberty subset issues and exceptionally attractive generic issues with mintages less than 5,000 coins probably have very bright futures.

• Buffalo gold has unreal design appeal to certain participants in the market. If the Mint does

2008-W $50 Mint State Gold Buffalo

in fact refuse to produce any more fractional proof and mint state gold Buffaloes the coins are going to do phenomenally well as one year type coins. The 2008-W $50 mint state gold Buffalo should do well either way. It's THE unbelievably deep relative rarity key to the ongoing $50 mint state denomination. In fact it's the rarest one ounce gold issue to come out of the U.S. Mint since 1933.

• The $5 uncirculated gold commemorative market has effectively been cornered by those with very "strong hands," and the set is nearing price maturity early as a result. The large percentage price growth is nearly over.

2004-2005 Westward Journey Nickels

Platinum

• Proof and mint state platinum Eagles with changing reverses are the high-end expression of the design driven series seen in circulation today. If you think that the collectors who are growing up picking through pocket change building what the Mint calls "collector series" with changing reverses like 50 state quarters, state parks quarters, life of Lincoln type pennies, Native American dollars, Presidential dollars, Westward Journey nickels etc., will carry that preference with them as they migrate to higher end material then you need to take a look at what more than likely will be regarded as the greatest "collector series" issued in almost half our coinage history.

Platinum Eagles by the Mint's own admission are unusual in that they have enjoyed complete thematic and design freedom allowing them to come up with consistently attractive designs without the interference of special interest groups. The high intrinsic value of platinum, which is over 10 times rarer than gold, has suppressed sales volumes over the lifetime of the program. *This set represents, as of this writing, the 14 rarest design-based proofs and the 11 rarest mint state type coins issued to the general public since 1915. The changing reverse platinum Eagles are the design-based rarity ranking for almost half our coinage history and for the moment they trade for just over melt!*

If the Mint closes the door on all the fractional changing reverse platinum Eagles as they have suggested in a effort to reduce their bloated product offerings, improve inventory turnover rates and avoid exposure to continued costly material volatility like they experienced in 2008, then the closed fractional platinum sets may well be the greatest collecting opportunity seen in our lifetime and indeed our grandparent's lifetime. The $100 changing reverse Eagles may also prove to be a great set. Coin historians may look back on them as the greatest type set issued from 1916 to 2016, but its road to coinage glory will likely be a harsh one and its keys like the 1929 to 1933 Saints before them may be a product of destruction or mishandling not just low initial mintages.

"No one after drinking old wine desires new wine for they say the old is better, but new wine must be put in new wine skins." The established collectors in 1900 had to be flexible enough to throw off the preconceptions of the past in order to embrace the fantastic date and mintmark opportunities moderns presented from 1906 to 1936. Historic collecting opportunities are again presenting themselves. *Are you willing* to see them?

CHAPTER 13

A $60 TRILLION WIND AT YOUR COLLECTION'S BACK

The Importance of Ultra Long Cycle Taxable Events

There have been numerous well-written studies in the last five years detailing the extreme seriousness of our Federal budget and national trade deficits and their consequences for us and our children. Unfortunately, the writers of these texts are not easily dismissed profits of doom out in the woods someplace, but top Federal accountants eminating from Federal Reserve Banks, the GAO and the Congressional Budget Office. *They have clearly demonstrated for us that* total taxation burdens are going up dramatically and as a consequence *we should be focusing at least part of our efforts on paying our taxes now* under the currently existing mild taxation rates, actively avoiding most deferred taxation schemes that don't have a substantial employer match *and placing our savings in anything we can find that has long-term real value growth prospects and does not create "taxable events."*

Let's look at some of the numbers that are scaring the government accountants to death and how high material content rare moderns can help us.

As of May 2009 our explicit federal liabilities (on books debt) was $11.25 trillion. The CBO analysis of President Obama's budget indicates that it will add $9.23 trillion to our current national debt load by 2019 and that's if universal health care is not enacted. Before the dramatic absorption of debt associated with the financial crisis that started in 2008, U.S. Comptroller General David Walker presented a 2007 dated report called GAO-08-446CG in which he estimated the "fiscal gap" associated with unfunded retirement benefits promised the Baby Boomers and other retirees to have a present value of approximately $40.8 trillion.

Current on Books Debt = $11.25 Trillion
CBO 2009 Projected Increase in Debt from 2010 to 2019 = $9.23 Trillion
GAO 2007 Estimated Unfunded Retirement Liability = $40.8 Trillion

By stacking up off-the-books debt, taxpayers over the last 40 years or so have enjoyed relatively mild income tax rates. We are reaching the point that our huge "off the books" obligations are about to move "on the books." Allan Greenspan recently said, "How governments finesse the transfer of real resources from shrinking shares of their populations who make up their work force to a growing retirement population is likely to be the defining question of the next quarter century." (Age of Turbulence, page 412)

RESPECTED FEDERAL EMPLOYEES HAVE GIVEN US OPTIONS SUCH AS:
1. Increase income tax rates 100 percent.
2. Eliminate all discretionary spending, including national defense.
3. Cut retirement transfer payments by 50 percent.
4. Impose emissions related cap and trade taxes equal to 20 percent of GDP.
5. Borrow heavily and monetize the debt by the modern equivalent of printing money to keep the real-term value of the debts workable.
6. Some combination of the above.

It's so bad that in report number GAO-06-1138CG, the Government Accountability Office called the Federal government a "burning platform." It was kind enough to outline in the same document how as a share of GDP Federal revenues are going to increase near term. It states on page 5: "In addition to the expiration of tax cuts, revenue as a share of GDP will increase ... due to (1) real bracket creep, (2) more taxpayers becoming subject to alternative minimum tax, and (3) increased revenue from tax-deferred retirement accounts." The Feds are in no position to give anyone any breaks. So we can reasonably expect:

A) THE BUSH TAX CUTS ARE LIKELY TO BE ALLOWED TO EXPIRE at some point because it requires no legislative action, and we can't afford them.

B) REAL TAX RATES WILL RISE DUE TO BRACKET CREEP. Greenspan feels like we can expect a core inflation rate of about 5 percent going forward. Tax rates are not indexed to inflation, so even with that conservative estimate we can expect today's $90,000 paycheck to see tax burdens intended for those making over $178,000 in 15 years. Based on 2000 tax law, that's the 36 percent marginal tax bracket and higher than today's 35 percent imposed on those making over $373,000 annually. Taxes intended for the "rich" are going to hit the middle class incrementally over time ... if we are lucky.

C) TAX DEFERRED RETIREMENT ACCOUNTS—THE TAXMAN'S TIME MACHINE
Tax deferred retirement programs are saving accounts for the government because our tax liability is not indexed to inflation and most of our Social Security benefit is going to be taxable if our 401K has any size once Federal mandated minimum withdrawals start. It's so easy to forget that Social Security is already effectively "means tested" by allowing it to count as taxable income above a very low threshold and other expensive governmental programs are likely to follow suit. Other than the contribution made by your employer, the 401K program is likely to be an open-ended taxation liability for the productive. Based on how much off-the-books debt the Federal government has been taking on we "should" have been paying much higher tax rates than we have been. *Income that has not or is not taxed at a rate high enough to cover current on- and off-the-books obligations is lost permanently from the Federal government's perspective if it is spent. If the current lower tax rate income is saved in any tax deferred format,*

the necessary high tax rate can be imposed later. If the savings are invested in anything that creates a long-term series of cash flows then the government will receive regular follow on taxable event opportunities.

Lower tax rate income that is invested in real estate equity, precious metals or rare high value items can grow without producing taxable events for a very long time, and they are resistant to the invisible tax we call inflation. The problem with most forms of collectibles is they do not enjoy a closely spaced intrinsic value floor that protects their holders from the specter of poor liquidity markets. Real estate can also go illiquid on you in a bad market, is subject to property tax and it frequently must be sold to divide it among heirs.

D) CARBON DIOXIDE EMISSIONS APPEAR TO BE EVOLVING INTO A POTENTIAL CORPORATE TAX BONANZA THAT CAN BE IMPOSED ON EVERYTHING THAT IS MANUFACTURED. If this energy-based tax policy is imposed on corporate America, ultimately it's imposed on the citizens, but the electorate may not see its as such immediately.

One unintended effect of high-energy prices is high mining cost. A quality ore body for gold or platinum yields one ounce for every 40 tons of rock. The total cost of extraction and processing is the long-term price floor under our metals purchases.

E) FEDERAL BORROWING COMBINED WITH MONEY CREATION TO BUY IT KNOWN AS DEBT MONETIZATION and the creeping inflation associated with it is almost certain to be one of the tools used to keep the real value of the public and private debts manageable.

CHAPTER 14

A $60 TRILLION WIND AT YOUR COLLECTION'S BACK

Shielding the Children with Heirlooms

Very successful individuals are lucky to receive 70 cents on the dollar after income taxes and from that will come another 50 cents on the dollar in the form of inheritance tax beyond whatever unindexed to inflation exemption is allowed at the time. That's approximately a 70 percent Federal marginal tax rate from the time a dollar is earned to the time it ends up in your children's or grandchildren's hands and that does not even consider State obligations. The handwriting is on the wall and it's up to us to begin the process of paying our taxes now and restructuring a portion of our assets beyond what we need to live on into alternatives whose ownership do not create taxable events for an extremely long period of time and tend to have equally long appreciation cycles.

It takes time to move family wealth without getting hit with unnecessary tax burdens. Why not contact your tax professional and make the most of currently existing gift exemptions for worthy younger relatives every year to help them through what David Walker says is likely to be "fiscal child abuse?"

If we change course and eliminate any unmatched deferred taxation contributions and instead use some of that after-tax income to gift young family members on a consistent basis with well-chosen relatively new coinage that is on the front end of the maturation cycle and they hold it until they are old, then the Federal government may not have the opportunity to capitalize on the value of that portion of the family estate again for 50 years or more. The family in this case is hit for today's payroll deductions and that's all. Well-chosen rare coins can easily pull hard for 50 years and not produce taxable events in the interim. Welcome to the estate saving power of ultra long cycle taxable events.

UNLIKE SO MANY ASSETS, A FINE MODERN COIN COLLECTION WITH HIGH MATERIAL CONTENT:

- Is not someone else's liability and as such cannot be defaulted on.
- Is not impacted by inflation or foreign investors willingness to hold dollars.
- Can appreciate in constant dollar terms for 30-50 years as the series mature.
- Can be held almost indefinitely.
- Is not subject to property tax.
- Offers excellent liquidity.
- Normally survives bankruptcy.
- Serves as an invisible form of wealth.
- Minimizes the impact of means testing.
- Can be exchanged in large or small increments.
- Is an enjoyable form of long-term savings.

THE TREASURY MADE THIS STATEMENT ON ITS PUBLIC AFFAIRS WEB SITE:

"Precious metals, precious stones, and jewels constitute easily transportable, highly concentrated forms of wealth. They serve as international mediums of exchange that can be converted into cash anywhere in the world. In addition, precious metals, especially gold, silver, and platinum, have a ready, actively traded market, and can be melted and poured into various forms, thereby obliterating refinery marks and leaving them virtually untraceable."

– Proposed Rule, 31 CFR Part 103, RIN 1506-AA28, Page 5

Coupling very long appreciation cycles with children's youth is good policy. Taking long term physical possession of part of your families assets in this way minimizes the potential influence of those that do not have your financial best interest at heart and puts a solid fire wall into your children's financial future that will likely endure regardless of how bad the budget and trade deficits get.

Thomas Jefferson would likely share our concern for the young and our over dependence on a fiat issuing Federal Bank. He commented:

"The democracy will cease to exit when you take away from those who are willing to work and give to those who would not."

"It is incumbent on every generation to pay its own debts as it goes. A principle which if acted on would save one-half the wars of the world."

"I predict future happiness for Americans if they prevent government from wasting the labors of the people under the pretense of taking care of them."

"I believe that banking institutions are more dangerous to our liberties than standing armies. If the American people ever allow private banks to control the issue of their currency, first by inflation, then by deflation, the banks and corporations that will grow around the banks will deprive the people of all property until their children wake-up homeless on the continent their fathers conquered."

CHAPTER 15

SELF-DIRECTED IRAS

The Opportunities and Pitfalls

2010 is a special year for successful individuals making over $100,000 a year who wish to participate in IRA programs that are funded from after-tax dollars for two reasons. First, the relatively mild Bush income tax rates are set to expire Dec. 31, 2010. Second, starting in 2010 higher income earners can convert their traditional IRAs to Roth IRAs and, equally importantly, spread the taxes due on the conversion over a two-year time span. Now is an excellent time to take a critical look at IRA participation and how it relates to modern coins struck on the precious metals.

There has been a growing public interest in self-directed IRAs with gold coinage held as one of its major components. Numerous organizations are attempting to cater to this market.

THERE ARE TWO PRIMARY TYPES OF MARKETERS IN THIS FIELD:

1. Organizations that effectively operate as coin dealers that tend to present the whole IRA process as one so they are able to push a transaction through their custodian and depository of choice quickly.

2. IRA custodians that will invest in anything that falls under the federal parameters and that just happens to include certain precious metal coins.

Unfortunately, many, but not all, of the first class of IRA marketers have the tendency to create an environment either directly or indirectly that puts their customers' savings at risk. This inordinate risk is produced by two practices:

1. Currently many organizations are herding their customer's savings into modern proof gold and have driven the retail price of these common coins up about 125 percent in 2009 alone by effectively causing IRA participants to compete with one another in a thin market for relatively common issues.

2. Genuinely scarce series keys available at a low to moderate mark-up over melt by and large are not recommended by IRA marketers because they can't "get enough of it to promote."

See the section on common high grade coins and promotions under "Common Pitfalls" starting on page 80.

AVOIDING IRA DRIVEN PRICE SPIKES IN COINAGE MARKETS

In January 2009 one ounce $50 proof gold Eagles could be purchased for about $1,100 each with ease. Almost over night dealers started paying $1,400 each for the same coin because many IRA marketers were paying $1,500 for them and selling the coins for anywhere between $1,600 and $2,500 each to their growing number of customers. This kind of price spike was also seen in the four-coin proof gold sets.

One of the major considerations that makes these very common coins worth holding is the floor afforded them by their intrinsic value. If you are paying twice melt for non-key date material then you have effectively ruined your bullion floor and paid key date prices for coins with very little numismatic future.

MAKING THE MOST OUT OF YOUR SELF-DIRECTED IRA

There are many large self-directed IRA custodians that are more than willing to purchase on your behalf precisely what you instruct them to and send the items to an approved depository provided they fall under Federally accepted parameters.

Those making such purchases may wish to consider doing some or all of the following:

1. *Attend at least one of the many free online self-directed IRA seminars.* Numismatic Guarantee Corporation (NGC) in conjunction with Entrust New Direction (a self-directed IRA custodian) has one of the better presentations.

2. *Develop a grocery list of the coins that you would like to own and educate yourself* on the current market. As mentioned previously, *Numismatic News* does an excellent job of keeping collectors up to date on the latest U.S. Mint cumulative weekly sales report. (See Appendix D) That weekly report alone is worth the cost of the annual subscription. The *Coin Dealer* newsletter, otherwise known as the "Grey Sheet," (copy designation 3B covers moderns) is the leading price list and you should buy one if you are actively accumulating better date coins.

3. *Buy from respected low margin modern coin dealers* that carry the rare sometimes hard to find material. Dealers like those listed in Appendix B can normally come up with whatever you are looking for.

4. *Avoid any U.S. gold coin trading much over 1.3 times melt value with a population of 30,000 or greater. Proof platinum Eagles with mintages over 10,000 should also be shunned if the seller is asking over 1.3 times intrinsic value.* Mint state platinum eagles with mintages over 7,000 coins are strictly a bullion play for raw or MS-69 issues and should be priced accordingly. Many internet IRA marketers promote this material because they can "get enough of it to promote" and that's precisely the reason you don't want be the buyer paying 1.5-2.5 times intrinsic value for such common material.

The reason we should avoid paying more than 1.3 times melt for modern Eagles is that the Mint sells proof and mint state gold Eagles directly to the public at about 1.3 times melt. So instead of paying

$1,750-$2,500 for a $50 common date proof gold Eagle, why not wait for the U.S. Mint to start its normal sales cycle and buy an identical coin of similar mintage for $1,300? The same thing is true of the $100 proof platinum Eagles and $1 silver Eagles.

Your self-directed IRA provider can place an order with the Mint on your behalf by sending a check overnight to:

United States Mint
POB 71191
Philadelphia PA 19176-6191

The Mint's prices are subject to change each Wednesday so it may be a good idea to start your order activity on Thursday so your order shows up in the then current pricing window. A complete description of the coin(s) along with its three-digit item code will be needed. Don't forget to add the $5 needed to cover freight. The Mint ordering service can be contacted at 1-800-USA-MINT or their Web site at www.usmint.gov.

5. Gold Eagles with sub 20,000 mintages, proof platinum Eagles with sub 7,000 mintages and mint state platinum Eagles with mintages less than 5,000 coins are worthy holdings. ***Older key date issues bringing twice melt or better should be purchased in mint state or proof 69 holders and then cracked out by the dealer and sent to NGC for "authentication holders" with serial numbers.*** This improves the likelihood that your key date Eagle is in acceptably high grade and you will know the coin sent to you when you pull it out of your IRA is your high-grade example. IRA holdings are not allowed to have a grade on the holder so "authentication" is the best available option.

6. Once you have picked out the coins and the dealer, give your custodian the specifics needed to make your purchase.

7. Make certain to specify to your chosen custodian that you want the depository selected to ***keep your holdings segregated***, otherwise you will be sending in rare modern coinage only to get back common material.

Dismiss the confiscation rhetoric that is so prevalent in the IRA marketing efforts. It is an attempt to move your price tolerance well above intrinsic value so they can over bill you for common high-grade coins new or old. There is no substitute for buying low mintage quality material at competitive prices.

DEFINING THE RATIOS

This is primarily a study of mintages, relative rarity and the resulting market prices. Each column in the graph represents single production year mintage sorted in descending order. The dates are listed but are not relevant. The blue line represents the prices paid by the market at each supply (mintage) level. The left Y-axis defines the mintages and right Y-axis denotes market prices.

The mean (middle) coin in terms of mintage is the 1939 half with a mintage of 8,808 and market price of about $800. This is the typical coin in the series in terms of value and rarity.

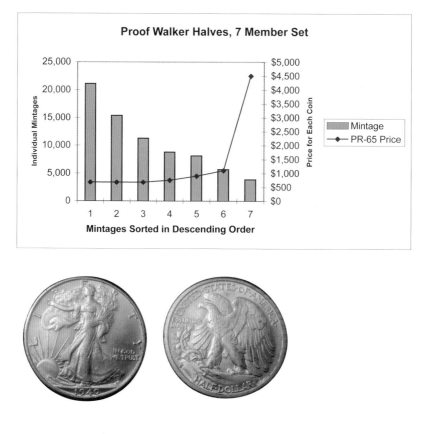

Proof Walking Liberty Halves

Year	Mintage	PR-65 Price
1942	21,120	$700
1941	15,412	$700
1940	11,279	$700
1939	8,808	$800
1938	8,152	$950
1937	5,728	$1,200
1936	3,901	$4,500
Totals	74,400	$9,550

As mentioned previously, the primary determining factor in a key coin's value is the number of collectors pursuing a series, their financial strength and the relative scarcity of the key date compared to its siblings. This is where some simple ratios shed light on the potential associated with a specific key date. Let's take a look at them.

Total series population to key coin ratio	19.1
Ratio of mean mintage to key coin	2.3
Ratio of second key to key date mintage	1.5
Ratio of key coin value to mean	6.0
Key coins price as fraction of whole set	0.48

TOTAL SERIES POPULATION TO KEY COIN RATIO. This is the total number of proof Walking Liberty halves struck between 1936 and 1942 divided by the mintage of the key 1936 half. 74,400/3901 = 19.1 This gives us some idea of how many common coins are out in the marketplace building collector interest in the key coin. Every common date in the hands of the public is a small advertisement for the key.

RATIO OF MEAN MINTAGE TO KEY COIN. This is a general measure of how rare the key is in relationship to the typical coin in the series. The 1939 mean mintage divided by the key date mintage is 8,808/3,901 = 2.3

RATIO OF SECOND KEY COIN TO KEY DATE MINTAGE. The second key date is the primary challenger to the key coin for leadership in the series. In this case the 1937 half with its 5,728 mintage divided by the 1936 half with its 3,901 mintage gives us about 1.47. A rather shallow advantage. When this ratio is low it tends to put a damper on the next very important ratio.

RATIO OF KEY COIN VALUE TO MEAN. Coin series in general have an exceedingly wide price range depending on material content, total series type rarity, etc. This ratio allows us to develop a feel for where key dates of certain mintage demographics tend to end up relative to the members of their own series. There is a high direct correlation between the total series population to key coin ratio, second key date to key date mintage ratio and the key coin value to mean ratio at the time of series maturity. ***Bottom line, if there is a huge series population and the key is much rarer than the next lowest mintage coin then the key will bring a very high multiple of the typical coin's price at maturity.*** In this case 1936 Walkers have a mild key coin value to mean ratio of $4,500/$800 = 6.0.

KEY COIN PRICE AS FRACTION OF WHOLE SET. This is the key coin's price divided by the total price of the set. In the current example, that's $4,500/$9,550 equaling .48. Obviously, if the key is worth 90 percent of the value of the entire set then there is probably little room to grow. On the other hand if a key date has a very high second key to key date mintage ratio and the fraction of whole set ratio is very low, great percentage growth can be expected.

MODERN COIN DEALERS USED BY THE AUTHOR

This is a listing of the coin dealers that I have used over the years that have given me good problem free service and their inclusion in no way ensures that your experience with them will be as positive (I have not been compensated in any way by those listed). When you call dealers, bear in mind Hank Swain's sage advice that "it's the absence of coins" that make an issue great, not the label. Moderns dealers like labels because it inflates their margins. Finding rare, attractive coinage at a competitive price is the goal.

Dealer	Contact	Specialization
John Rothans	714-746-8085	Large volume only, $10,000 minimum
Modern Coin Mart	800-362-9004	Small & large volume - General
Robert Lecce	561-483-4744	Small & large volume - General
Mitchell Spivack	949-394-7122	Platinum and Gold Eagles
First Coin Source	702-443-8822	Small volume - General
GNS Eagles	317-670-6092	Small volume - General
RM Trading	800-850-4143	W mint marked gold
Sherman Coins	732-597-3195	Silver Eagles
Strashnick Coins	401-738-6022	General
Eric Jordan-Buyers Agent	678-982-0934	Market Research

ENABLING LEGISLATION

The original legislation creating the coins we collect as expressed primarily in U.S. Code Title 31 sets the parameters of what the U.S. Mint can and can't do in regard to material content, design change, production levels and program duration. In short, we can look at the enabling legislation and get some excellent clues about what a set of coins is going to look like in final form. It's helpful to know:

1. How long can the series run?
2. Will the series have a large total population?
3. Will the set be collected by series date and mintmark?
4. Will the coins be regarded as a type set?
5. Is the Mint likely go from a stable design on both sides to a changing reverse thus modifying what is regarded as the key?

It is important to have some idea of where we are going before we get there. Let's look at some of the legislation that is likely to impact the active series.

Platinum Eagle Enabling Legislation Paraphrased:

Public Law 104-208

U.S. Code Title 31,5112 k

The Secretary may mint and issue platinum bullion coins and proof platinum coins in accordance with such specifications, designs, varieties, quantities, denominations and inscriptions as the secretary, in the Secretary's discretion, may prescribe from time to time.

Furthermore the Secretary is authorized to use Government platinum reserves stockpiled at the United States Mint as working inventory and shall ensure that reserves utilized are replaced by the Mint.

THE BOTTOM LINE FOR PLATINUM EAGLES *is the Secretary has almost total freedom in regard to thematic, design, and physical characteristics for any platinum coins.* Producing platinum Eagles in any form is completely optional and production does not have to meet public demand. Director Moy stated on Sept. 19, 2007, at the "Art of the Metal" conference in Colorado Springs, "I want to spark a new awakening of design excellence in coin design,and embody the American spirit in new and renewed allegorical or iconic symbolism. The 24-karat ... programs are a golden opportunity for this. After the first year, 24k gold and platinum designs are not dictated by Congress." Despite cost overruns and the Mint's clearly stated intention to eliminate platinum fractional issues, we can reasonably expect platinum Eagles to survive in some form because they offer the Mint the opportunity to be creative.

Gold Eagle Enabling Legislation Paraphrased:

Public Law 99-185, Gold Bullion Act of 1985

U.S. Code Title 31, Section 5112 i

The Secretary shall mint and issue gold coins described below in quantities sufficient to meet public demand:
- A fifty dollar coin that is 32.7mm in diameter, weighs 33.931 grams and contains one troy ounce of fine gold.
- A twenty-five dollar coin that is 27mm in diameter, weighs 16.966 grams and contains one-half troy ounce of fine gold.
- A ten-dollar coin that is 22mm in diameter, weighs 8.483 grams and contains one-forth troy ounce of fine gold.
- A five-dollar coin that is 16.5mm in diameter, weighs 3.393 grams and contains one-tenth ounce of fine gold.
- The gold coins shall have a design determined by the Secretary, except that the fifty dollar gold coin shall have on the obverse side a design symbolic of liberty and on the reverse side a design representing a family of eagles, with the male carrying an olive branch back to the nest.

The Secretary shall acquire gold for the coins under this title from domestic mines within one year of being produced. The Secretary shall not pay more than the average world price for the gold. In the absence of available supplies of such gold the Secretary may use gold from reserves held by the United States to mint the coins.

The Secretary shall make bulk sales of the gold coins minted under this subsection at a price equal to their material content value plus all direct and indirect cost including overhead.

U.S. Code 31, 5112 (d) 2 States that the Secretary may change the design of a coin only once within 25 years of the first adoption of the design, model, hub or die for that coin unless otherwise instructed by Congress.

THE BOTTOM LINE FOR 92 PERCENT FINE GOLD EAGLES is the Mint is supposed to strike and sell in bulk quantities 22-karat gold coins from domestic mines in volumes large enough to meet public demand in four denominations. The series is subject to the 25-year design change limitation and thus the gold Eagles are not open to revision until 2011 under normal circumstances. A new design can be selected at that time if the Secretary sees, fit but the design will be stable again for another 25-year run thereafter. When the Mint's legal department was asked if any exceptions to the 25-year design stability rule could be interpreted from current law for these coins the answer was "none that have been tested yet." Director Moy's comments also clearly indicate that the 25-year design stability law applies.

Unless the law or its current interpretation changes, 92 percent gold Eagle issues are highly likely to be collected by series date and mint-mark. Under current law there is not going to be enough design variety for the collector base to view the set as a series collected principally by type especially with the already massive single design populations continuing to grow at a annual rate sufficient "to meet public demand."

Buffalo Gold Enabling Legislation Paraphrased:

Public Law 109-145, $1 Presidential Coin Act of 2005

U.S. Code Title 31, Section 5112 q

A $50 gold coin that is of appropriate size and thickness, as determined by the Secretary, weighs 1 ounce, and contains 99.99 percent pure gold shall be produced not later than 6 months after the date of the enactment of the presidential $1 Coin Act of 2005. The Secretary shall commence striking and issuing for sale such number of $50 gold bullion and proof coins as the Secretary may determine to be appropriate, in such quantities, as the Secretary, in the Secretary's discretion, may prescribe.

The obverse and reverse of the gold bullion coins struck under this subsection during the first year of issuance shall bear the 1913 Type 1 Buffalo designs by James Fraser. After the first year of issue the Secretary may change the obverse or reverse design after consulting with the commission of fine arts and the Citizens Coinage Advisory Committee.

The Secretary shall acquire gold for the coins under this title from domestic mines within one year of being produced. The Secretary shall not pay more than the average world price for the gold. In the absence of available supplies of such gold the Secretary may use gold from reserves held by the United States to mint the coins.

U.S. Code Title 31,5122 (i) 4 C

The Secretary may issue other bullion and proof coins under this subsection in accordance with such designs, varieties, quantities, and denominations as the secretary, in the Secretary's discretion, may prescribe from time to time.

THE BOTTOM LINE FOR .999 FINE GOLD is the Mint is supposed to strike proof and business strike $50 coins on pure gold produced from domestic mines every year. The first year must be based on the Buffalo nickel, but after that the design is up to the Mint and they can change it every year if they want to. Production quantities are not required to be "struck to demand" and so unlike business strike gold eagle production the Mint can set production limits as they see fit. The decision to strike or not strike fractional pure gold coinage is up to the Mint. The Mint is offered an unusual degree of design and thematic freedom under this legislation. Mint Director Moy on March 20th 2008 at the Artistic Infusion Symposium in Philadelphia said, "We have unlimited design opportunities with our 24-karat gold and platinum coins. Let us not waste those opportunities." The Type I Buffalo design on .999 fine gold is likely going to be a relatively short set even for the $50 denomination.

Commemorative Program General Limitations Paraphrased:
U.S. Code Title 31, Section 5112 m

Beginning Jan.1, 1999, the Secretary may mint and issue not more than two commemorative coin programs in any single calendar year. Furthermore, the Secretary shall not mint more than 750,000 mint state and proof clad half dollars as a combined total, not more than 500,000 mint state and proof silver dollars as a combined total and not more than 100,000 mint state and proof gold five or ten dollar coins as a combined total.

If, however, the Secretary determines based on independent, market-based research conducted by the special interest recipient of the commemorative surcharges that the mintage levels described are not adequate to meet public demand then the Secretary may waive one or more of the mintage limits with respect to the commemorative program in question.

THE BOTTOM LINE FOR THE COMMEMORATIVES is Congress abused the program in the mid-1990s and came out with more offerings than the collector base could absorb and mintages crashed. Congress was trying to self-limit itself though the use of guidelines.

Silver Eagles Enabling Legislation Paraphrase:

Public Law 99-61, Liberty Coin Act of 1985

U.S. Code Title 31, Section 5112 e

The Secretary shall mint and issue, in quantities sufficient to meet public demand coins which are 40.6 mm in diameter, weigh 31.103 grams, contain .999 fine silver, have a design symbolic of liberty on the obverse side, an eagle on the reverse side and have reeded edges. Its denomination shall be $1.

Silver eagles shall be issued in bulk and the sales price for the coins shall be equal to the price of bullion at the time plus the cost of minting, marketing and distribution of such coins.

U.S. Code 31, 5112 (d) 2 States that the Secretary may change the design of a coin only once within 25 years of the first adoption of the design, model, hub or die for that coin unless otherwise instructed by Congress.

THE BOTTOM LINE FOR SILVER EAGLES is the Mint is supposed to strike and sell in bulk quantities .999 fine silver dollars in volumes large enough to meet public demand. The series is subject to the 25-year design change limitation and thus the Silver Eagles are not subject to revision until 2011. A new design can be selected at that time if the Secretary sees fit but the design will likely be stable again for another 25-year run thereafter.

Unless the law changes or how it is currently interpreted does, silver Eagle issues are highly likely to be collected by series date and mintmark. Unless the law or its current interpretation changes there is not going to be enough design variety for the collector base to view the set as a series collected principally by type especially with the already massive single design populations continuing to grow at a annual rate sufficient "to meet public demand."

First Spouse Enabling Legislation Paraphrased:

Public Law 109-145, Presidential $1 Coin Act of 2005

U.S. Code Title 31, Section 5112 o

During the same period as the Presidential dollars are being produced the Secretary shall issue proof and uncirculated gold coins under this subsection that are emblematic of the spouse of each such President. The coins issued under this subsection shall have the same diameter as the $1 coins, weigh .5 ounce and contain .999 fine gold.

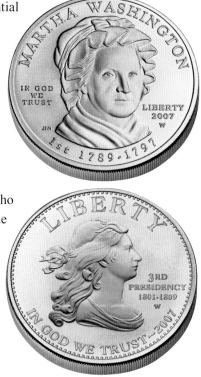

THE COIN'S OBVERSE SHALL CONTAIN:

1. The name and likeness of a person who was a spouse of a President during the Presidents period of service.
2. An inscription of the years during which such person was the spouse of a President during the Presidents years of service.
3. A number indicating the order of the period of service in which such President served.
4. An image emblematic of the concept of liberty as represented on a United States coin issued during the period of the President's tenure if he did not serve with a wife.
5. In the case of Chester A. Arthur, the image of Alice Paul, a leading strategist in the women's suffrage movement.

THE REVERSE DESIGN SHALL BEAR:

1. Images of the life and work of the First Spouse.
2. The inscription "The United States of America" and the denomination of $10.
3. A design representative of the themes of the President if he did not serve with a wife.
4. In the case of Chester Arthur, a suffrage movement theme.

A separate coin shall be designed and issued for each person who was the spouse of a President during any portion of the term of office of such President.

The Secretary shall prescribe the maximum number of coins that shall be issued with each of the designs selected and announce before the issuance the maximum number of that design that will be issued. The Secretary shall purchase newly mined domestic gold for use in the coins and charge a price for the coins equal to or greater than the sum of the face value of the coins and the cost of designing and issuing including all overhead.

THE BOTTOM LINE FOR THE FIRST SPOUSE SERIES is the set will be a product of political compromises and most of the thematic and design consistency needed to foster set cohesion are going to be absent. The coins are likely to develop under the behavior described under the unstable design models section. Design appeal may be almost as important as mintage in some cases.

The Mint will finish out the program regardless of how few sell. They are free to chose the maximum number to be issued and must declare it in advance. This will be a long, costly series to complete and it is likely to have some of the lowest mintage gold seen in the last 100 years among its members due to its structural problems.

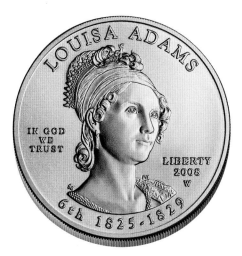

Presidential Dollars Enabling Legislation Paraphrased:

Public Law 109-145, Presidential $1 Coin Act of 2005

U.S. Code Title 31, Section 5112 n

One dollar coins issued beginning Jan.1, 2007, shall have an obverse with the name and likeness of a President of the United States, basic information about the president including the dates or years of the term in office and a number indicating the order of service. The coins obverse shall bear a likeness of the Statue of Liberty extending to the rim of the coin and large enough to provide a dramatic representation of Liberty while not being large enough to create the impression of a 2-headed coin. The obverse shall have the inscription $1 and United States of America but the word Liberty shall be absent because the Statue of Liberty adequately conveys the concept. The year of the minting or issuance of the coin and the inscriptions "E Pluribus Unum" and "In God We Trust" shall be Edge Incused.

The coins issued under this subsection commemorating Presidents shall be issued in the order of the period of service and only one coin design shall be issued for any President no matter how many consecutive terms of office the President served. If a President has served during 2 or more nonconsecutive periods of service, a coin shall be issued under this subsection for each such period. Four Presidents a year shall be honored until all Presidents dead for at least 2 years have been represented and then may not be resumed except by an Act of Congress. Upon termination of this program the design of all $1 coins shall revert to the so called "Sacagawea-design" $1 coins.

The Secretary may mint and issue such number of $1 coins of each design selected under this subsection in uncirculated and proof form as the Secretary determines to be appropriate.

THE BOTTOM LINE FOR PRESIDENTIAL DOLLARS is the Mint must strike a stable Statue of Liberty reverse series with a changing Presidential obverse at the rate of four per year. The Secretary can produce proofs but it is not required. All quantity limits are to be set by the Secretary. In the end the Presidential dollar series will be a type set composed of about 40 different members struck at multiple mints.

Sacagawea Enabling Legislation Paraphrased:

Public Law 110-82, Native American Coin Act of 2008

U.S. Code Title 31, Section 5112 r

Secretary shall mint and issue $1 coins that have the Sacagawea obverse design and a annually changing reverse design that celebrates important Indian Contributions to the development and history of the United States. The inscriptions of the year of minting and E Pluribus Unum shall be edge-incused.

The reverse designs shall be chosen by the Secretary after consultation with the Committee on Indian Affairs of the Senate, the Congressional Native American Caucus of the House of Representatives, the Commission of Fine Arts, the National Congress of American Indians and the Citizens Coinage Advisory Committee. The reverse may depict individuals and events such as:

1. The creation of the Cherokee written language.
2. The Iroquois Confederacy.
3. Wampanoag Chief Massasoit.
4. The Pueblo Revolt.
5. Olympian Jim Thorpe.
6. Ely S Park, a general on the staff of Ulysses S. Grant and later head of the Bureau of Indian Affairs.
7. Code Talkers who served the US Armed Forces during World War I and II.

Each coin issued shall be in chronological order in which the Native Americans lived or events occurred until the termination of the companion Presidential dollar program. Thereafter the reverse designs shall be issued in any order considered appropriate by the Secretary after consolation with the above mentioned Native American groups. Sacagawea design dollars shall represent not less than 20 percent of total "golden dollar" production (this is a reduction from the previous one-third requirement). Proofs may be issued as the Secretary deems appropriate.

THE BOTTOM LINE FOR SACAGAWEA DOLLARS is its likely to be a large series with high total population and a great deal of design variety. Collecting by reverse design will likely be the dominant collection structure at maturity for this series.

National Parks Quarters Enabling Legislation Paraphrased:

Public Law 110-456, National Parks Quarter Act of 2008

U.S. Code Title 31, Section 5112 t

Quarters issued beginning in 2010 shall have designs on the reverse emblematic of the significant national sites in the States, District of Columbia and of the territories of the United States. The selection of a national park reverse or other national site in each state shall be made by the Secretary of the Treasury after consultation with the Secretary of the Interior, the chief executive of each state, the Commission of Fine Arts, and the Citizens Coinage Advisory Committee. No head and shoulders of any person living or dead or outline of map of a State may be included on the reverse.

Five designs shall be issued every year until all states and territories have been so honored. The Secretary may make the determination to have a second round of special sites honored in each State or Territory. The Secretary shall determine the quantities of each coin to be issued. The Secretary may mint and issue such number of uncirculated and proof quarter dollars as the Secretary determines to be appropriate.

The Secretary may mint and issue such number of quarter dollars of each above design as the Secretary determines to be appropriate in 90 percent silver and 10 percent copper.

Upon the completion of the coin program under this subsection the obverse of the quarter dollar shall revert to the same design containing the image of President Washington in effect for the quarter prior to the 50 State Quarter Program and the reverse shall contain an image of General Washington crossing the Delaware River prior to the Battle of Trenton.

THE BOTTOM LINE FOR THE NATIONAL PARKS QUARTERS is the Washington quarter series will include between 115 and 171 different reverse designs by 2031 under existing legislation. Design is destined to be the dominant collecting format for the Washington quarter set at some point. Ninety percent silver quarters in mint state and proof form are authorized but their issuance is left up to the discretion of the Secretary.

Ultra High Relief Gold Enabling Legislation Paraphrased:

U.S. Code Title 31,
Section 5112 i 4 c

The Secretary may continue to mint and issue coins in accordance with existing law (strike 22 karat gold Eagles, .999 fine $50 Buffalo gold and .999 fine First Spouse $10 gold) and at the same time mint and issue other bullion and proof gold coins in accordance with such programs, procedure, specifications, designs, varieties, quantities, denominations and inscriptions as the Secretary, in the Secretary's discretion, may prescribe from time to time.

The Mint's allies in Congress attempted to enact specific Public Law calling for a single year run of the Ultra High Relief $20 Gold followed by a Palladium coin to take its place after the first year but the bill did not pass. Consequently Mint Director Moy had to request authority from the Secretary to strike the Ultra High Relief gold. It was granted under the above general authority.

THE BOTTOM LINE FOR ULTRA HIGH RELIEF GOLD is the Secretary is not facing any direct guidelines from Congress and the only thing that prevents the Secretary and the Mint from producing a multiple year run of this coin is their publicly stated intentions not to.

Five-Ounce Silver National Parks Investment Product Enabling Legislation Paraphrased:

Public Law 110-456, National Parks Quarter Act of 2008
U.S. Code Title 31, Section 5112 u

The Secretary shall strike and sell such number of bullion coins as the Secretary determines to be appropriate that are exact duplicates of the State Parks Program quarters each of which shall:

A) Have a diameter of 3.0 inches and a weight of 5.0 ounces.

B) Contain .999 fine silver.

C) Have incused into the edge the fineness and weight.

D) Bear the inscription quarter dollar.

E) Not be minted or issued as so called fractional coins or in any size other than the size described in (A).

F) Only be available for sale during the year that its sibling circulating quarter dollar is issued.

In addition to the authorized dealers normally utilized by the Secretary in distributing bullion coins and solely for the purposes of distributing coins issued under this subsection, the director of the National Park Service may purchase these coins in lots of at least 1,000 and resell or repackage them as the director determines to be appropriate.

THE BOTTOM LINE IS THE 5-OUNCE SILVER BULLION COINS are going to be special issues that offer the sites being honored the opportunity to earn surcharges by buying in bulk from the Mint and selling retail. The series will have 56 or 112 members at the time of termination assuming none of the territories secede. It will be a large high intrinsic value set that offers obverse design cohesion as well as reverse design variety.

Congress allows no net losses on special issue coins.

U.S. Code Title 31, Section 5112

The Secretary shall take all action necessary to ensure that the issuance of the coins minted under this section (5112 of title 31) shall result in no net cost to the United States Government.

THE BOTTOM LINE FOR MODERN NON-CIRCULATING COINAGE is a voluntary series that consistently looses money will not survive. This is one of the reasons fractional gold and platinum Eagles with mintmarks were suspended after the 2008 production year.

TRENDS IN THE U.S. MINT'S WEEKLY SALES REPORT

The Mint publishes every Tuesday or Wednesday what it calls the "weekly sales report" for its current numismatic offering that is closely followed by many who take an interest in moderns.

The report represents the number of cumulative orders taken through what is normally Monday of that week. This is not perfectly representative of the number of coins shipped because:

1. It does not necessarily include the impact of mint cancellations of orders.

2. It does not always reflect the coins that have or will be returned under the 7 day return option granted the buyers.

3. Orders can be taken beyond the number of coins in stock by a fairly wide margin to cover potential returns from customers.

Despite all this ***the report has a long history of being correct within 10 percent of final mintage the vast majority of the time.*** This is especially true if the issue's final week isn't a violent sell out.

Let's take a look at how a new coin's cumulative sales usually progress if it is offered to the public over a majority of the year and does not have any special mintage or buyer limitations placed on it that are meaningful.

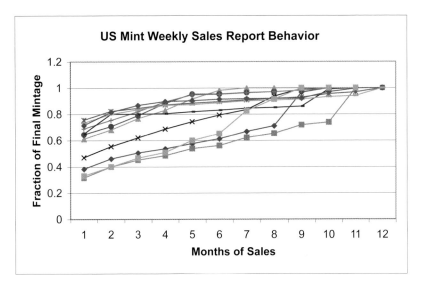

US Mint Weekly Sales Report Behavior

Notice many coins sell great for a few months and then sales flatten out or the Mint runs out of coins. Others start out the year soft and tend to see sales spike hard near the end of the sales period. With that said there is one very important rule of thumb that this chart reveals to us.

In almost every case over the last 10 years the Mint will sell at least 40 percent of what will be the final mintage of the coin in question in the first eight weeks. So we can safely assume most of the time that *no more than 2.5 times the eight weeks sales number will exist in the public's hands at the end of the year.*

MASTER MINTAGE LISTINGS FOR PROOF EAGLES

Proof Platinum Eagle Mintages

Year/ Reverse Design	$100	$50	$25	$10
1997 Eagle Over Sun	20,851	15,431	18,628	36,993
1998 New England	14,912	13,836	14,873	19,847
1999 Wet Lands	12,363	11,103	13,507	19,133
2000 Heart Land	12,453	11,049	11,995	15,651
2001 South West	8,969	8,254	8,847	12,174
2002 North West	9,834	8,772	9,282	12,365
2003 Patriotic Vigilance	8,246	7,131	7,044	9,534
2004 Seated America	6,007	5,063	5,193	7,161
2005 Plenty	6,602	5,942	6,592	8,104
2006 Legislative	9,152	7,649	7,813	10,205
2007 Executive	8,363	22,873	6,017	8,176
2007 Executive Reverse Proof	-	16,937	-	-
2008 Judicial	4,769	4,020	4,153	5,138
2009 Perfect Union	8,000	* -	-	-

Proof First Spouse Gold

Year	$10
2007 Washington	19,167
2007 Adams	17,149
2007 Jefferson	19,815
2007 Madison	17,943
2008 Monroe	7,800
2008 Adams	6,581
2008 Jackson	7,684
2008 Van Buren	7,364*
2009 Harrison	

Above are last minute updates not reflected in text.

* Estimates

Proof Gold Eagle Mintages

Year	$50	$25	$10	$5
1986	446,290	-	-	-
1987	147,498	143,398	-	-
1988	87,133	76,528	98,028	143,881
1989	54,570	44,798	54,170	84,647
1990	62,401	51,636	62,674	99,349
1991	50,411	53,125	50,839	70,334
1992	44,826	40,976	46,269	64,874
1993	34,369	31,130	33,775	45,960
1994	46,674	44,584	48,172	62,849
1995	46,368	45,388	47,526	62,667
1996	36,153	35,058	38,219	57,047
1997	28,034	26,344	29,805	34,977
1998	25,886	25,374	29,503	39,395
1999	31,427	30,427	34,417	48,428
2000	33,007	32,028	36,036	49,971
2001	24,555	23,240	25,613	37,530
2002	27,499	26,646	29,242	40,864
2003	28,344	28,270	30,292	40,027
2004	28,215	27,330	28,839	35,131
2005	35,246	34,311	37,207	49,265
2006	47,000	34,322	36,127	47,277
2006 Rev Proof	9,996	-	-	-
2007	51,810	44,025	46,189	58,553
2008	30,237	22,602	18,877	28,116

Proof Gold Buffalo Mintages

Year	$50	$25	$10	$5
2006	246,267	-	-	-
2007	58,998	-	-	-
2008	18,863	12,169	13,125	18,884
2009	50,000	-	-	-

Proof Silver Eagles

Year	$1
1986	1,446,778
1987	904,732
1988	557,370
1989	617,694
1990	695,510
1991	511,924
1992	498,543
1993	405,913
1994	372,168
1995	407,822
1995-W	30,102
1996	498,293
1997	440,315
1998	450,728
1999	549,330
2000	600,743
2001	746,398
2002	647,342
2003	747,831
2004	801,602
2005	816,663
2006	1,092,475
2006-RP	248,875
2007	821,759
2008	700,979
2009	-

MASTER MINTAGE LISTINGS FOR MINT STATE EAGLES

Business Strike Platinum Eagles

Year	$100	$50	$25	$10
1997 Eagle Over the Sun	56,000	20,500	27,100	70,250
1998 Eagle Over the Sun	133,002	32,419	38,887	39,525
1999 Eagle Over the Sun	56,707	32,309	39,734	55,955
2000 Eagle Over the Sun	10,003	18,892	20,054	34,027
2001 Eagle Over the Sun	14,070	12,815	21,815	52,017
2002 Eagle Over the Sun	11,502	24,005	27,405	23,005
2003 Eagle Over the Sun	8,007	17,409	25,207	22,007
2004 Eagle Over the Sun	7,009	13,236	18,010	15,010
2005 Eagle Over the Sun	6,310	9,013	12,013	14,013
2006 Eagle Over the Sun	6,000	9,602	12,001	11,001
2007 Eagle Over the Sun	7,202	7,001	8,402	13,003
2008 Eagle Over the Sun	21,800	14,000	22,800	17,000

Changing Reverse Mint State Platinum Eagles

	$100	$50	$25	$10
2006-W Legislative	3,068	2,577	2,676	3,544
2007-W Executive	4,177	3,635	3,690	5,556
2008-W Judicial	2,876	2,253	2,481	3,706

Mint State Gold Eagles

Year	$50	$25	$10	$5
1986	1,362,650	599,566	726,031	912,609
1987	1,045,500	131,255	269,255	580,266
1988	465,500	45,000	49,000	159,500
1989	415,790	44,829	81,789	264,790
1990	373,219	31,000	41,000	210,210
1991	243,100	24,100	36,100	165,200
1992	275,000	54,404	59,546	209,300
1993	480,192	73,324	71,864	210,709
1994	221,663	62,400	72,650	206,380
1995	200,636	53,474	83,752	223,025
1996	189,148	39,287	60,318	401,964
1997	664,508	79,605	108,805	528,515
1998	1,468,530	169,029	309,829	1,344,520
1999	1,505,026	263,013	564,232	2,750,338
1999-W	-	-	< 6,000	6,000
2000	433,319	79,287	128,964	569,153
2001	143,605	48,047	71,280	269,147
2002	222,029	70,027	62,027	230,027
2003	416,032	79,029	74,029	245,029
2004	417,019	98,040	72,014	250,016
2005	356,555	80,023	72,015	300,043
2006	237,510	66,005	60,004	285,006
2006-W	45,053	15,164	15,188	20,643
2007	140,016	47,002	34,004	190,010
2007-W	18,608	11,455	12,766	22,501
2008	710,000	61,000	70,000	305,000
2008-W	11,908	15,683	8,883	12,657
2009	1,315,500	110,000	110,000	270,000

Mint State Buffalo Gold

Year	$50	$25	$10	$5
2006	337,012	-	-	-
2007	136,503	-	-	-
2008	189,500	-	-	-
2008-W	9,074	16,908	9,949	17,429
2009	200,000			

Mint State First Spouse Gold

Year	$10
2007 Washington	17,661
2007 Adams	17,142
2007 Jefferson	19,823
2007 Madison	12,340
2008 Monroe	4,462
2008 Adams	3,885
2008 Jackson	4,609
2008 Van Buren	4,191*
2009 Harrison	*

Above are last minute updates not reflected in text.

Mint State Silver Eagles

Year	$1
1986	5,393,005
1987	11,442,335
1988	5,004,646
1989	5,203,327
1990	5,840,110
1991	7,191,066
1992	5,540,068
1993	6,763,762
1994	4,227,319
1995	4,672,051
1996	3,603,386
1997	4,295,004
1998	4,847,547
1999	7,408,640
2000	9,239,132
2001	9,001,711
2002	10,539,026
2003	8,495,008
2004	8,882,754
2005	8,891,025
2006	10,676,522
2006-W	466,573
2007	9,028,036
2007-W	690,891
2008	20,583,000
2008-W	535,000
2008-W/07 reverse	47,000
2009	28,766,500
2009 W	

* Estimates

MASTER MINTAGE LISTINGS
FOR MODERN COMMEMORATIVES

Proof Silver Dollars

1983S Discus	1,577,025
1984S Los Angeles	1,801,210
1986S Statue of Liberty	6,414,638
1987S Constitution	2,747,116
1988S Olympics	1,359,366
1989S Congress Bicentennial	762,198
1990P Eisenhower	1,144,461
1991P Korea	618,488
1991S Mount Rushmore	738,419
1991S USO	321,275
1992P Columbus	385,241
1992W White House	375,849
1992S XXV Olympiad	504,505
1993S Bill of Rights	534,001
1993S Thomas Jefferson	332,891
1993W World War II	342,041
1994P POW	220,100
1994S US Capital	279,416
1994P Vietnam	226,262
1994P Women in Military	213,201
1994S World Cup	576,978
1995S Civil War	437,114
1995P Gymnastics	182,676
1995P Paralympics	138,337
1995P Special Olympics	351,764
1995P Track & Field	136,935
1996S Community Service	101,543
1996P Cycling	118,795
1996P High Jump	124,502
1996P Rowing	151,890
1996P Smithsonian	129,152
1996P Tennis	92,016
1996P Wheel Chair	84,280
1997P Botanic Garden	264,528

Proof Silver Dollars *continued*

1997S Jackie Robinson	110,495
1997P Law Enforcement	110,428
1998S Black War Patriot	75,070
1998S Robert Kennedy	99,020
1999P Dolley Madison	224,403
1999S Yellowstone	128,646
2000P Library of Congress	196,900
2000P Lief Ericson	144,748
2001P Buffalo	272,869
2001P Capital Visitor Center	143,793
2002P Salt Lake City	166,864
2002W West Point	288,293
2003P First Flight	193,086
2004P Edison	213,409
2004P Lewis & Clark	288,492
2005P John Marshall	141,993
2005P Marine	548,810
2006P Franklin Founding	136,037
2006P Franklin Scientist	137,808
2006S San Francisco	255,700
2007P Desegregation	124,678
2007P Jamestown	258,802
2008P Bald Eagle	243,558
2009P Braille	135,000
2009P Lincoln	375,000

Mint State Silver Dollars

1983P Los Angeles	294,543
1983D Los Angeles	174,014
1983S Los Angeles	174,014
1984P Olympic	217,954
1984D Olympic	116,675
1984S Olympic	116,675
1986P Statue of Liberty	723,635
1987P Constitution	451,629
1988D Olympiad	191,368
1989D Congress	135,203
1990W Eisenhower	241,669
1991P Mount Rushmore	133,139
1991D Korean War	213,049
1991D USO	124,958
1992D XXV Olympiad	187,552
1992D Columbus	106,949
1992D White House	123,803
1993D Bill of Rights	98,383
1993D WWII	94,708
1994D World Cup	81,698
1993P Jefferson Silver	266,927
1994W Vietnam	57,317
1994W POW	54,790
1994W Women Service	53,054
1994D Capital	68,352
1995P Civil War	45,866
1995D Gymnastics	42,497
1995D Paralympics	28,649
1995D Track and Field	24,976
1995D Cycling	19,662
1996D Tennis	15,983
1996D High Jump	15,697
1996D Wheelchair	14,497
1996D Rowing	16,258
1995W Special Olympics	89,301
1996S Community Service	23,500
1996D Smithsonian	31,230
1997P Botanic Garden	57,272
1997S Jackie Robinson	30,007
1997P Law Enforcement	28,575
1998S Robert Kennedy	106,422
1998S Black Patriots	37,210
1999P Dolly Madison	89,104

Mint State Silver Dollars *continued*

1999P Yellowstone	23,614
2000P Library Of Congress	52,771
2000P Leif Erickson	28,150
2001D American Buffalo	227,100
2001P Visitor Center	35,400
2002P Salt Lake City	40,257
2002W West Point	103,201
2003P First Flight	53,761
2004P Thomas Edison	68,051
2004P Lewis and Clark	90,323
2005P John Marshall	48,953
2005P Marine Corps	49,671
2006P Franklin-Scientist	61,956
2006P Franklin-Founder	64,014
2006S San Francisco	65,609

Proof $5 Gold

1986 Statue of Liberty	404,013
1987 Constitution	651,659
1988 Olympiad	281,465
1989 Congress Bic.	164,690
1991 Mount Rushmore	111,991
1992 XXV Olympiad	77,313
1992 Columbus	79,730
1993 Bill of Rights	78,651
1993 World War II	65,461
1994 World Cup	89,614
1995 Civil War	55,246
1995 Torch Runner	57,442
1995 Stadium	43,124
1996 Flag Bearer	32,886
1996 Cauldron	38,555
1996 Smithsonian	21,840
1997 Jackie Robinson	24,072
1997 Roosevelt	29,233
1999 Washington	41,693
2001 Capital Visitor	27,652
2002 Salt Lake	32,877
2006 San Francisco Mint	41,517
2007 Jamestown	47,050
2008 Bald Eagle	59,000

Mint State $5 Gold

1986 Liberty	95,248
1987 Constitution	214,225
1988 Olympiad	62,913
1989 Congress	46,899
1991 Rushmore	31,959
1992 Olympiad	27,732
1992 Columbus	24,329
1993 Bill of Rights	23,266
1993 World War II	23,089
1994 World Cup	22,464
1995 Civil War	12,735
1995 Torch Runner	14,675
1995 Stadium	10,579
1996 Flag	9,174
1996 Cauldron	9,210
1996 Smithsonian	9,068
1997 Jackie R.	5,174
1997 FDR	11,894
1999 Washington	22,511
2001 Visitor Center	6,761
2002 Salt Lake	10,585
2006 Old Mint	16,230
2007 Jamestown	18,843
2008 Bald Eagle	13,467

Mint State Dollars

2007P Central High	66,093
2007P Jamestown	79,801
2008P Bald Eagle	110,073
2009P Lincoln	*125,000
2009P Braille	* 83,000

COMMEMORATIVE COINAGE 1982-PRESENT

All commemorative silver dollar coins of 1982-present have the following specifications: diameter — 38.1 millimeters; weight — 26.7300 grams; composition — 0.9000 silver, 0.7736 ounces actual silver weight. All commemorative $5 coins of 1982-present have the following specificiations: diameter — 21.6 millimeters; weight — 8.3590 grams; composition: 0.9000 gold, 0.242 ounces actual gold weight.

Note: In 1982, after a hiatus of nearly 20 years, coinage of commemorative half dollars resumed. Those designated with a 'W' were struck at the West Point Mint. Some issues were struck in copper-nickel. Those struck in silver have the same size, weight and composition as the prior commemorative half-dollar series.

HALF DOLLAR

George Washington, 250th Birth Anniversary.
KM# 208 Obv. Designer: Elizabeth Jones **Obverse:** George Washington on horseback facing **Reverse:** Mount Vernon **Diameter:** 30.6 **Weight:** 12.5000 g. **Composition:** 0.9000 Silver, 0.3617 oz. ASW.

Date	UNC Mintage	Proof Mintage	MS-65	Prf-65
1982D	2,210,458	—	7.75	—
1982S	—	4,894,044	—	7.75

Statue of Liberty Centennial.
KM# 212 Obv. Designer: Edgar Z. Steever **Rev. Designer:** Sherl Joseph Winter **Obverse:** State of Liberty and sunrise **Reverse:** Emigrant family looking toward mainland **Weight:** 11.3400 g. **Composition:** Copper-Nickel Clad Copper

Date	UNC Mintage	Proof Mintage	MS-65	Prf-65
1986D	928,008	—	5.25	—
1986S	—	6,925,627	—	4.95

Congress Bicentennial.
KM# 224 Obv. Designer: Patricia L. Verani

Rev. Designer: William Woodward and Edgar Z. Steever **Obverse:** Statue of Freedom head **Reverse:** Capitol building **Weight:** 11.3400 g. **Composition:** Copper-Nickel Clad Copper

Date	UNC Mintage	Proof Mintage	MS-65	Prf-65
1989D	163,753	—	7.50	—
1989S	—	762,198	—	7.25

Mount Rushmore 50th Anniversary.
KM# 228 Obv. Designer: Marcel Jovine **Rev. Designer:** T. James Ferrell **Reverse:** Mount Rushmore portraits **Weight:** 11.3400 g. **Composition:** Copper-Nickel Clad Copper

Date	UNC Mintage	Proof Mintage	MS-65	Prf-65
1991D	172,754	—	19.50	—
1991S	—	753,257	—	18.50

1992 Olympics.
KM# 233 Obv. Designer: William Cousins **Rev. Designer:** Steven M. Bieda **Obverse:** Torch and laurel **Reverse:** Female gymnast and large flag **Weight:** 11.3400 g. **Composition:** Copper-Nickel Clad Copper

Date	UNC Mintage	Proof Mintage	MS-65	Prf-65
1992P	161,607	—	8.50	—
1992S	—	519,645	—	9.00

Columbus Voyage - 500th Anniversary.

KM# 237 Designer: T. James Ferrell. **Obverse:**
Columbus standing on shore **Reverse:** Santa Maria
sailing right **Weight:** 11.3400 g. **Composition:**
Copper-Nickel Clad Copper

Date	UNC Mintage	Proof Mintage	MS-65	Prf-65
1992D	135,702	—	11.50	—
1992S	—	390,154	—	10.50

James Madison - Bill of Rights.

KM# 240 Obv. Designer: T. James Ferrell
Rev. Designer: Dean McMullen **Obverse:** James
Madison writing, Montpelier in background
Reverse: Statue of Liberty torch **Weight:** 12.5000 g.
Composition: 0.9000 Silver, 0.3617 oz. ASW.

Date	UNC Mintage	Proof Mintage	MS-65	Prf-65
1993W	193,346	—	18.50	—
1993S	—	586,315	—	15.00

World War II 50th Anniversary.

KM# 243 Obv. Designer: George Klauba
Rev. Designer: William J. Leftwich **Obverse:** Three
portraits, plane above, large V in background
Reverse: Pacific island battle scene **Weight:**
11.3400 g. **Composition:** Copper-Nickel Clad
Copper

Date	UNC Mintage	Proof Mintage	MS-65	Prf-65
(1993)P	197,072	—	24.50	—
(1993)P	—	317,396	—	23.50

1994 World Cup Soccer.

KM# 246 Obv. Designer: Richard T. LaRoche
Rev. Designer: Dean McMullen **Obverse:** Soccer
player with ball **Reverse:** World Cup 94 logo
Weight: 11.3400 g. **Composition:** Copper-Nickel
Clad Copper

Date	UNC Mintage	Proof Mintage	MS-65	Prf-65
1994D	168,208	—	9.00	—
1994P	122,412	—	10.25	—
1994P	—	609,354	—	8.00

1996 Atlanta Olympics - Baseball.

KM# 262 Obv. Designer: Edgar Z. Steever
Obverse: Baseball batter at plate, catcher and
umpire **Reverse:** Hemisphere and Atlanta Olympics
logo **Weight:** 11.3400 g. **Composition:** Copper-
Nickel Clad Copper

Date	UNC Mintage	Proof Mintage	MS-65	Prf-65
1995S	164,605	—	20.50	—
1995S	—	118,087	—	18.00

1996 Atlanta Olympics - Basketball.

KM# 257 Obverse: Three players, one jumping for
a shot **Reverse:** Hemisphere and Atlanta Olympics
logo **Weight:** 11.3400 g. **Composition:** Copper-
Nickel Clad Copper

Date	UNC Mintage	Proof Mintage	MS-65	Prf-65
1995S	171,001	—	19.00	—
1995S	—	169,655	—	16.00

Civil War Battlefield Preservation.

KM# 254 Obv. Designer: Don Troiani
Rev. Designer: T. James Ferrell **Obverse:** Drummer
and fenceline **Reverse:** Canon overlooking
battlefield **Weight:** 11.3400 g. **Composition:**
Copper-Nickel Clad Copper

Date	UNC Mintage	Proof Mintage	MS-65	Prf-65
1995S	119,510	—	39.50	—
1995S	—	330,099	—	38.50

U. S. Capitol Visitor Center.

KM# 323 Obv. Designer: Dean McMullen
Rev. Designer: Alex Shagin and Marcel Jovine
Obverse: Capitol sillouete, 1800 structure in detail
Reverse: Legend within circle of stars **Weight:**
11.3400 g. **Composition:** Copper-Nickel Clad Copper

Date	UNC Mintage	Proof Mintage	MS-65	Prf-65
2001P	99,157	—	13.50	—
2001P	—	77,962	—	15.50

1996 Atlanta Olympics - Soccer.

KM# 271 Obverse: Two female soccer players
Reverse: Atlanta Olympics logo **Weight:** 11.3400 g.
Composition: Copper-Nickel Clad Copper

Date	UNC Mintage	Proof Mintage	MS-65	Prf-65
1996S	52,836	—	138	—
1996S	—	122,412	—	100.00

First Flight Centennial.

KM# 348 Obv. Designer: John Mercanti
Rev. Designer: Donna Weaver **Obverse:** Wright
Monument at Kitty Hawk **Reverse:** Wright Flyer in
flight **Weight:** 11.3400 g. **Composition:** Copper-
Nickel Clad Copper

Date	UNC Mintage	Proof Mintage	MS-65	Prf-65
2003P	57,726	—	15.00	—
2003P	—	109,710	—	16.00

1996 Atlanta Olympics - Swimming.

KM# 267 Obverse: Swimmer right in butterfly
stroke **Reverse:** Atlanta Olympics logo **Weight:**
11.3400 g. **Composition:** Copper-Nickel Clad
Copper

Date	UNC Mintage	Proof Mintage	MS-65	Prf-65
1996S	49,533	—	150	—
1996S	—	114,315	—	34.50

American Bald Eagle.

KM# 438 Obverse: Two eaglets in nest with egg
Reverse: Eagle Challenger right, American Flag in
background **Diameter:** 30.6 **Weight:** 11.3400 g.
Composition: Copper-Nickel Clad Copper

Date	UNC Mintage	Proof Mintage	MS-65	Prf-65
2008P	120,000	—	10.00	—
2008P	—	175,000	—	15.00

1984 Los Angeles Olympics - Discus.
KM# 209 Obv. Designer: Elizabeth Jones
Obverse: Trippled discus thrower and five star logo
Reverse: Eagle bust left

Date	UNC Mintage	Proof Mintage	MS-65	Prf-65
1983P	294,543	—	17.50	—
1983D	174,014	—	18.50	—
1983S	174,014	—	18.50	—
1983S	—	1,577,025	—	18.00

Statue of Liberty Centennial.
KM# 214 Obv. Designer: John Mercanti
Rev. Designer: John Mercanti and Matthew Peloso
Obverse: Statue of Liberty and Ellis Island great hall
Reverse: State of Liberty torch

Date	UNC Mintage	Proof Mintage	MS-65	Prf-65
1986P	723,635	—	17.80	—
1986S	—	6,414,638	—	18.50

1984 Los Angeles Olympics - Stadium Statues.
KM# 210 Obv. Designer: Robert Graham **Obverse:**
Statues at exterior of Los Angeles Memorial Coliseum
Reverse: Eagle standing on rock

Date	UNC Mintage	Proof Mintage	MS-65	Prf-65
1984P	217,954	—	17.50	—
1984D	116,675	—	18.50	—
1984S	116,675	—	18.50	—
1984S	—	1,801,210	—	18.50

Constitution Bicentennial.
KM# 220 Obv. Designer: Patricia L. Verani
Obverse: Feather pen and document **Reverse:**
Group of people

Date	UNC Mintage	Proof Mintage	MS-65	Prf-65
1987P	451,629	—	17.80	—
1987S	—	2,747,116	—	18.50

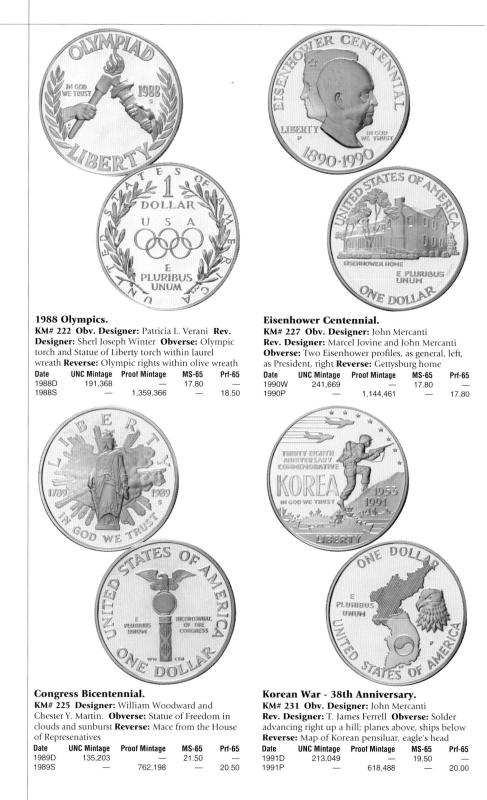

1988 Olympics.
KM# 222 Obv. Designer: Patricia L. Verani **Rev. Designer:** Sherl Joseph Winter **Obverse:** Olympic torch and Statue of Liberty torch within laurel wreath **Reverse:** Olympic rights within olive wreath

Date	UNC Mintage	Proof Mintage	MS-65	Prf-65
1988D	191,368	—	17.80	—
1988S	—	1,359,366	—	18.50

Eisenhower Centennial.
KM# 227 Obv. Designer: John Mercanti
Rev. Designer: Marcel Jovine and John Mercanti
Obverse: Two Eisenhower profiles, as general, left, as President, right **Reverse:** Gettysburg home

Date	UNC Mintage	Proof Mintage	MS-65	Prf-65
1990W	241,669	—	17.80	—
1990P	—	1,144,461	—	17.80

Congress Bicentennial.
KM# 225 Designer: William Woodward and Chester Y. Martin. **Obverse:** Statue of Freedom in clouds and sunburst **Reverse:** Mace from the House of Represenatives

Date	UNC Mintage	Proof Mintage	MS-65	Prf-65
1989D	135,203	—	21.50	—
1989S	—	762,198	—	20.50

Korean War - 38th Anniversary.
KM# 231 Obv. Designer: John Mercanti
Rev. Designer: T. James Ferrell **Obverse:** Solder advancing right up a hill; planes above, ships below **Reverse:** Map of Korean pensiluar, eagle's head

Date	UNC Mintage	Proof Mintage	MS-65	Prf-65
1991D	213,049	—	19.50	—
1991P	—	618,488	—	20.00

Mount Rushmore 50th Anniversary.
KM# 229 Obv. Designer: Marika Somogyi
Rev. Designer: Frank Gasparro **Obverse:** Mount
Rushmore portraits, wreath below **Reverse:** Great
seal in rays, United States map in background

Date	UNC Mintage	Proof Mintage	MS-65	Prf-65
1991P	133,139	—	28.50	—
1991S	—	738,419	—	23.50

1992 Olympics - Baseball.
KM# 234 Obv. Designer: John R. Deecken and
Chester Y. Martin **Rev. Designer:** Marcel Jovine
Obverse: Baseball pitcher **Reverse:** Shield flanked
by stylized wreath, olympic rings above

Date	UNC Mintage	Proof Mintage	MS-65	Prf-65
1992D	187,552	—	22.50	—
1992S	—	504,505	—	24.50

USO 50th Anniversary.
KM# 232 Obv. Designer: Robert Lamb
Rev. Designer: John Mercanti **Obverse:** USO
banner **Reverse:** Eagle pearched right atop globe

Date	UNC Mintage	Proof Mintage	MS-65	Prf-65
1991D	124,958	—	18.00	—
1991S	—	321,275	—	18.50

Columbus Discovery - 500th Anniversary.
KM# 238 Obv. Designer: John Mercanti
Rev. Designer: Thomas D. Rogers, Sr. **Obverse:**
Columbus standing with banner, three ships in
background **Reverse:** Half view of Santa Maria on
left, Space Shuttle Discovery on right

Date	UNC Mintage	Proof Mintage	MS-65	Prf-65
1992D	106,949	—	26.00	—
1992P	—	385,241	—	29.00

White House Bicentennial.

KM# 236 Obv. Designer: Edgar Z. Steever
Rev. Designer: Chester Y. Martin **Obverse:** White
House's north portico **Reverse:** John Hoban bust
left, main entrance doorway

Date	UNC Mintage	Proof Mintage	MS-65	Prf-65
1992D	123,803	—	26.00	—
1992W	—	375,851	—	28.00

Thomas Jefferson 250th Birth Anniversary.

KM# 249 Designer: T. James Ferrell. **Obverse:**
Jefferson's head left **Reverse:** Monticello home

Date	UNC Mintage	Proof Mintage	MS-65	Prf-65
1993P	266,927	—	18.50	—
1993S	—	332,891	—	19.50

James Madison - Bill of Rights.

KM# 241 Obv. Designer: William Krawczewicz
and Thomas D. Rogers, Sr. **Rev. Designer:** Dean
McMullen and Thomas D. Rogers, Sr.
Obverse: James Madison bust right, at left
Reverse: Montpelier home

Date	UNC Mintage	Proof Mintage	MS-65	Prf-65
1993D	98,383	—	18.50	—
1993S	—	534,001	—	20.50

World War II 50th Anniversary.

KM# 244 Designer: Thomas D. Rogers, Sr..
Obverse: Soldier on Normandy beach **Reverse:**
Insignia of the Supreme Headquarters of the AEF
above Eisenhower quote

Date	UNC Mintage	Proof Mintage	MS-65	Prf-65
1993D	94,708	—	29.50	—
1993W	—	342,041	—	37.50

1994 World Cup Soccer.
KM# 247 Obv. Designer: Dean McMullen and
T. James Ferrell **Rev. Designer:** Dean McMullen
Obverse: Two players with ball **Reverse:** World Cup
94 logo

Date	UNC Mintage	Proof Mintage	MS-65	Prf-65
1994D	81,698	—	22.50	—
1994S	—	576,978	—	23.50

U.S. Capitol Bicentennial.
KM# 253 Obverse: Capitol dome, Statue fo
Freedom surrounded by stars **Reverse:** Eagle on
shield, flags flanking

Date	UNC Mintage	Proof Mintage	MS-65	Prf-65
1994D	68,352	—	18.00	—
1994S	—	279,416	—	22.50

National Prisoner of War Museum.
KM# 251 Obv. Designer: Thomas Nielson and
Alfred Maletsky **Rev. Designer:** Edgar Z. Steever
Obverse: Eagle in flight left within circle of barbed
wire **Reverse:** National Prisioner of War Museum

Date	UNC Mintage	Proof Mintage	MS-65	Prf-65
1994W	54,790	—	85.00	—
1994P	—	220,100	—	42.00

Vietnam Veterans Memorial.
KM# 250 Obv. Designer: John Mercanti
Rev. Designer: Thomas D. Rogers, Sr.
Obverse: Outstretched hand touching names on the
Wall, Washington Monument in background
Reverse: Service Medals

Date	UNC Mintage	Proof Mintage	MS-65	Prf-65
1994W	57,317	—	79.00	—
1994P	—	226,262	—	65.00

Women in Military Service Memorial.
KM# 252 Obv. Designer: T. James Ferrell
Rev. Designer: Thomas D. Rogers, Sr.
Obverse: Five uniformed women left
Reverse: Memorial at Arlington National Cemetery

Date	UNC Mintage	Proof Mintage	MS-65	Prf-65
1994W	53,054	—	36.50	—
1994P	—	213,201	—	30.00

1996 Atlanta Olympics - Gymnastics.
KM# 260 Obverse: Two gymnast, female on floor exercise and male on rings **Reverse:** Two clasped hands, Atlanta Olypic logo above

Date	UNC Mintage	Proof Mintage	MS-65	Prf-65
1995D	42,497	—	67.50	—
1995P	—	182,676	—	50.00

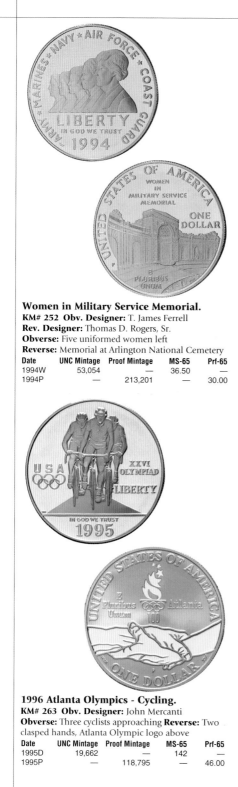

1996 Atlanta Olympics - Cycling.
KM# 263 Obv. Designer: John Mercanti
Obverse: Three cyclists approaching **Reverse:** Two clasped hands, Atlanta Olympic logo above

Date	UNC Mintage	Proof Mintage	MS-65	Prf-65
1995D	19,662	—	142	—
1995P	—	118,795	—	46.00

1996 Atlanta Olympics - Track and field.
KM# 264 Obv. Designer: John Mercanti **Obverse:** Two runners on a track, one crossing finish line **Reverse:** Two clasped hands, Atlanta Olympic logo above

Date	UNC Mintage	Proof Mintage	MS-65	Prf-65
1995D	24,796	—	92.00	—
1995P	—	136,935	—	49.00

1996 Atlanta Paralympics - Blind runner.
KM# 259 Obverse: Blind runner **Reverse:** Two clasped hands, Atlanta Olympic logo above

Date	UNC Mintage	Proof Mintage	MS-65	Prf-65
1995D	28,649	—	82.00	—
1995P	—	138,337	—	54.00

Special Olympics World Games.
KM# 266 Obv. Designer: Jamie Wyeth and T. James Ferrell **Rev. Designer:** Thomas D. Rogers, Sr. **Obverse:** Eunice Schriver head left; founder of the Special Olympics **Reverse:** Logo on medal, rose, quote

Date	UNC Mintage	Proof Mintage	MS-65	Prf-65
1995W	89,301	—	29.50	—
1995P	—	351,764	—	26.50

Civil War.
KM# 255 Obv. Designer: Don Troiani and Edgar Z. Steever **Rev. Designer:** John Mercanti **Obverse:** Solder giving water to wounded soldier **Reverse:** Chamberlain quote and battlefield monument

Date	UNC Mintage	Proof Mintage	MS-65	Prf-65
1995P	45,866	—	69.00	—
1995S	—	437,114	—	69.00

1996 Atlanta Olympics - High Jump.
KM# A272 Rev. Designer: Thomas D. Rogers, Sr. **Obverse:** High jumper

Date	UNC Mintage	Proof Mintage	MS-65	Prf-65
1996D	15,697	—	380	—
1996P	—	124,502	—	58.00

1996 Atlanta Olympics - Rowing.

KM# 272 Rev. Designer: Thomas D. Rogers, Sr.
Obverse: Four man crew rowing left **Reverse:**
Atlanta Olympic logo

Date	UNC Mintage	Proof Mintage	MS-65	Prf-65
1996D	16,258	—	345	—
1996P	—	151,890	—	70.00

1996 Atlanta Paralympics - Wheelchair racer.

KM# 268 Rev. Designer: Thomas D. Rogers, Sr.
Obverse: Wheelchair racer approaching with
uplifted arms **Reverse:** Atlanta Olympics logo

Date	UNC Mintage	Proof Mintage	MS-65	Prf-65
1996D	14,497	—	365	—
1996P	—	84,280	—	82.00

1996 Atlanta Olympics - Tennis.

KM# 269 Rev. Designer: Thomas D. Rogers, Sr.
Obverse: Female tennis player **Reverse:** Atlanta
Olympics logo

Date	UNC Mintage	Proof Mintage	MS-65	Prf-65
1996D	15,983	—	315	—
1996P	—	92,016	—	85.00

National Community Service.

KM# 275 Obv. Designer: Thomas D. Rogers, Sr.
Rev. Designer: William C. Cousins **Obverse:**
Female standing with lamp and shield **Reverse:**
Legend within wreath

Date	UNC Mintage	Proof Mintage	MS-65	Prf-65
1996S	23,500	—	220	—
1996S	—	101,543	—	76.00

Smithsonian Institution 150th Anniversary.
KM# 276 Obv. Designer: Thomas D. Rogers, Sr.
Rev. Designer: John Mercanti **Obverse:** Original
Smithsonian building, the "Castle" designed by
James Renwick **Reverse:** Female seated with torch
and scroll on globe

Date	UNC Mintage	Proof Mintage	MS-65	Prf-65
1996D	31,230	—	135	—
1996P	—	129,152	—	57.50

National Law Enforcement Officers Memorial.
KM# 281 Designer: Alfred Maletsky.
Obverse: Male and female officer admiring name on
monument **Reverse:** Rose on a plain shield

Date	UNC Mintage	Proof Mintage	MS-65	Prf-65
1997P	—	110,428	—	105
1997P	28,575	—	160	—

Jackie Robinson.
KM# 279 Obv. Designer: Alfred Maletsky
Rev. Designer: T. James Ferrell **Obverse:** Jackie
Robinson sliding into base **Reverse:** Anniversary logo

Date	UNC Mintage	Proof Mintage	MS-65	Prf-65
1997S	30,007	—	98.00	—
1997S	—	110,495	—	118

U.S. Botanic Gardens 175th Anniversary.
KM# 278 Designer: Edgar Z. Steever. **Obverse:**
National Botanic Gardens Conservatory building
Reverse: Rose

Date	UNC Mintage	Proof Mintage	MS-65	Prf-65
1997P	57,272	—	39.50	—
1997P	—	264,528	—	38.00

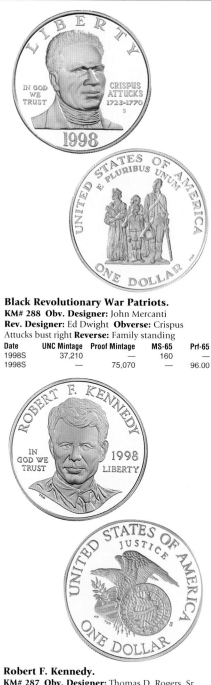

Black Revolutionary War Patriots.
KM# 288 Obv. Designer: John Mercanti
Rev. Designer: Ed Dwight **Obverse:** Crispus
Attucks bust right **Reverse:** Family standing

Date	UNC Mintage	Proof Mintage	MS-65	Prf-65
1998S	37,210	—	160	—
1998S	—	75,070	—	96.00

Dolley Madison.
KM# 298 Designer: Tiffany & Co.. **Obverse:**
Madison bust right, at left **Reverse:** Montpelier home

Date	UNC Mintage	Proof Mintage	MS-65	Prf-65
1999P	89,104	—	42.00	—
1999P	—	224,403	—	34.50

Robert F. Kennedy.
KM# 287 Obv. Designer: Thomas D. Rogers, Sr.
Rev. Designer: James M. Peed and Thomas D.
Rogers, Sr. **Obverse:** Kennedy bust facing **Reverse:**
Eagle on sheild, Senate Seal

Date	UNC Mintage	Proof Mintage	MS-65	Prf-65
1998S	106,422	—	31.50	—
1998S	—	99,020	—	42.50

Yellowstone.
KM# 299 Obv. Designer: Edgar Z. Steever
Rev. Designer: William C. Cousins **Obverse:** Old
Faithful gyser erupting **Reverse:** Bison and vista as
on National Parks shield

Date	UNC Mintage	Proof Mintage	MS-65	Prf-65
1999P	23,614	—	49.50	—
1999P	—	128,646	—	45.00

Leif Ericson.
KM# 313 Obv. Designer: John Mercanti
Rev. Designer: T. James Ferrell **Obverse:** Ericson bust helmeted right **Reverse:** Viking ship sailing left

Date	UNC Mintage	Proof Mintage	MS-65	Prf-65
2000P	28,150	—	87.00	—
2000 Iceland	15,947	—	—	25.00
2000P	144,748	—	—	70.00

Capitol Visitor Center.
KM# 324 Obv. Designer: Marika Somogyi
Rev. Designer: John Mercanti **Obverse:** Original and current Capital facades **Reverse:** Eagle with sheild and ribbon

Date	UNC Mintage	Proof Mintage	MS-65	Prf-65
2001P	35,400	—	30.00	—
2001P	—	143,793	—	39.00

Library of Congress Bicentennial.
KM# 311 Obv. Designer: Thomas D. Rogers, Sr.
Rev. Designer: John Mercanti **Obverse:** Open and closed book, torch in background **Reverse:** Skylight dome above the main reading room

Date	UNC Mintage	Proof Mintage	MS-65	Prf-65
2000P	52,771	—	38.00	—
2000P	—	196,900	—	33.00

Native American - Bison.
KM# 325 Designer: James E. Fraser. **Obverse:** Native American bust right **Reverse:** Bison standing left

Date	UNC Mintage	Proof Mintage	MS-65	Prf-65
2001D	227,100	—	175	—
2001P	—	272,869	—	180

2002 Winter Olympics - Salt Lake City.
KM# 336 Obv. Designer: John Mercanti
Rev. Designer: Donna Weaver **Obverse:** Salt Lake City Olympic logo **Reverse:** Stylized skyline with mountains in background

Date	UNC Mintage	Proof Mintage	MS-65	Prf-65
2002P	40,257	—	30.00	—
2002P	166,864	—	—	38.00

First Flight Centennial.
KM# 349 Obv. Designer: T. James Ferrell
Rev. Designer: Norman E. Nemeth
Obverse: Orville and Wilbur Wright busts left
Reverse: Wright Flyer over dunes

Date	UNC Mintage	Proof Mintage	MS-65	Prf-65
2003P	53,761	—	33.50	—
2003P	—	193,086	—	28.50

U.S. Military Academy at West Point - Bicentennial.
KM# 338 Obv. Designer: T. James Ferrell
Rev. Designer: John Mercanti **Obverse:** Cadet Review flagbearers, Academy buildings in background **Reverse:** Academy emblems - Corinthian helmet and sword

Date	UNC Mintage	Proof Mintage	MS-65	Prf-65
2002W	103,201	—	18.50	—
2002W	—	288,293	—	18.50

Lewis and Clark Corps of Discovery Bicentennial.
KM# 363 Obverse: Lewis and Clark standing
Reverse: Jefferson era clasped hands peace medal

Date	UNC Mintage	Proof Mintage	MS-65	Prf-65
2004P	90,323	—	31.00	—
2004P	—	288,492	—	27.50

Thomas A. Edison - Electric Light 125th Anniversary.

KM# 362 Obv. Designer: Donna Weaver
Rev. Designer: John Mercanti **Obverse:** Edison
half-length figure facing holding light bulb
Reverse: Light bulb and rays

Date	UNC Mintage	Proof Mintage	MS-65	Prf-65
2004P	68,031	—	34.00	—
2004P	—	213,409	—	34.50

John Marshall, 250th Birth Anniversary.

KM# 375 Obv. Designer: John Mercanti
Rev. Designer: Donna Weaver **Obverse:** Marshall
bust left **Reverse:** Marshall era Supreme Court
Chamber

Date	UNC Mintage	Proof Mintage	MS-65	Prf-65
2005P	67,096	—	32.00	—
2005P	—	196,753	—	35.00

U.S. Marine Corps, 230th Anniversary.

KM# 376 Obverse: Flag Raising at Mt. Suribachi on
Iwo Jima **Reverse:** Marine Corps emblem

Date	UNC Mintage	Proof Mintage	MS-65	Prf-65
2005P	49,671	—	37.00	—
2005P	—	548,810	—	39.00

Benjamin Franklin, 300th Birth Anniversary.

KM# 387 Obv. Designer: Norman E. Nemeth
Obverse: Youthful Franklin flying kite **Reverse:**
Revolutionary era "JOIN, or DIE" snake cartoon
illustration

Date	UNC Mintage	Proof Mintage	MS-65	Prf-65
2006P	61,856	—	32.00	—
2006P	—	137,808	—	45.00

Benjamin Franklin, 300th Birth Anniversary.

KM# 388 Obverse: Bust 3/4 right, signature in oval below **Reverse:** Continental Dollar of 1776 in center

Date	UNC Mintage	Proof Mintage	MS-65	Prf-65
2006P	64,014	—	33.00	—
2006P	—	137,808	—	44.00

Central High School Desegregation.

KM# 418 Rev. Designer: Don Everhart II
Obverse: Children's feet walking left with adult feet in military boots **Reverse:** Little Rock's Central High School

Date	UNC Mintage	Proof Mintage	MS-65	Prf-65
2007P	66,093	—	50.00	—
2007P	—	124,618	—	50.00

San Francisco Mint Museum.

KM# 394 Obv. Designer: Sherl J. Winter
Obverse: 3/4 view of building **Reverse:** Reverse of 1880s Morgan silver dollar

Date	UNC Mintage	Proof Mintage	MS-65	Prf-65
2006S	65,609	—	41.00	—
2006S	—	255,700	—	42.00

Jamestown - 400th Anniversary.

KM# 405 Obv. Designer: Donna Weaver
Rev. Designer: Don Everhart II **Obverse:** Two settlers and Native American **Reverse:** Three ships

Date	UNC Mintage	Proof Mintage	MS-65	Prf-65
2007P	79,801	—	36.50	—
2007P	—	258,802	—	35.00

American Bald Eagle.
KM# 439 Obverse: Eagle with flight, mountain in background at right **Reverse:** Great Seal of the United States

Date	UNC Mintage	Proof Mintage	MS-65	Prf-65
2008P	110,073	—	39.50	—
2008P	—	243,558	—	38.50

Lincoln Bicentennial.
KM# 454 Obv. Designer: Justin Kunz and Don Everhart II **Rev. Designer:** Phebe Hemphill **Obverse:** 3/4 portrait facing right **Reverse:** Part of Gettysburg Address within wreath

Date	UNC Mintage	Proof Mintage	MS-65	Prf-65
2009P	125,000	—	41.00	—
2009P	—	375,000	—	38.50

Louis Braille Birth Bicentennial.
KM# 455 Obv. Designer: Joel Iskowitz and Phebe Hemphill **Rev. Designer:** Susan Gamble and Joseph Menna **Obverse:** Louis Braille bust facing **Reverse:** School child reading book in Braille, BRL in Braille code above

Date	UNC Mintage	Proof Mintage	MS-65	Prf-65
2009P	82,639	—	32.50	—
2009P	—	135,235	—	42.50

$5 (HALF EAGLE)

Statue of Liberty Centennial.
KM# 215 Designer: Elizabeth Jones.
Obverse: Statue of Liberty head right **Reverse:** Eagle in flight left

Date	UNC Mintage	Proof Mintage	MS-65	Prf-65
1986W	95,248	—	330	—
1986W	—	404,013	—	330

Constitution Bicentennial.
KM# 221 Designer: Marcel Jovine. **Obverse:** Eagle left with quill pen in tallion **Reverse:** Upright quill pen

Date	UNC Mintage	Proof Mintage	MS-65	Prf-65
1987W	214,225	—	330	—
1987W	—	651,659	—	330

1988 Olympics.
KM# 223 Obv. Designer: Elizabeth Jones
Rev. Designer: Marcel Jovine **Obverse:** Nike head wearing olive wreath **Reverse:** Stylized olympic couldron

Date	UNC Mintage	Proof Mintage	MS-65	Prf-65
1988W	62,913	—	330	—
1988W	—	281,456	—	330

Congress Bicentennial.
KM# 226 Obv. Designer: John Mercanti
Obverse: Capitol dome **Reverse:** Eagle atop of the canopy from the Old Senate Chamber

Date	UNC Mintage	Proof Mintage	MS-65	Prf-65
1989W	46,899	—	330	—
1989W	—	164,690	—	330

Mount Rushmore 50th Anniversary.
KM# 230 Obv. Designer: John Mercanti
Rev. Designer: Robert Lamb and William C. Cousins **Obverse:** Eagle in flight towards Mount Rushmore **Reverse:** Legend at center

Date	UNC Mintage	Proof Mintage	MS-65	Prf-65
1991W	31,959	—	395	—
1991W	—	111,991	—	345

1992 Olympics.
KM# 235 Obv. Designer: James C. Sharpe and T. James Ferrell **Rev. Designer:** James M. Peed **Obverse:** Sprinter, U.S. Flag in background **Reverse:** Heraldic eagle, olympic rings above

Date	UNC Mintage	Proof Mintage	MS-65	Prf-65
1992W	27,732	—	395	—
1992W	—	77,313	—	345

Columbus Quincentenary.
KM# 239 Obv. Designer: T. James Ferrell **Rev. Designer:** Thomas D. Rogers, Sr. **Obverse:** Columbust profile left, at right, map of Western Hemisphere at left **Reverse:** Arms of Spain, and parchment map

Date	UNC Mintage	Proof Mintage	MS-65	Prf-65
1992W	24,329	—	395	—
1992W	—	79,730	—	345

James Madison - Bill of Rights.
KM# 242 Obv. Designer: Scott R. Blazek **Rev. Designer:** Joseph D. Peña **Obverse:** Madison at left holding document **Reverse:** Eagle above legend, torch and laurel at sides

Date	UNC Mintage	Proof Mintage	MS-65	Prf-65
1993W	23,266	—	435	—
1993W	—	78,651	—	345

World War II 50th Anniversary.
KM# 245 Obv. Designer: Charles J. Madsen **Rev. Designer:** Edward S. Fisher **Obverse:** Soldier with expression of victory **Reverse:** Morse code dot-dot-dot-dash for V, large in background; V for Victory

Date	UNC Mintage	Proof Mintage	MS-65	Prf-65
1993W	23,089	—	465	—
1993W	—	65,461	—	385

1994 World Cup Soccer.
KM# 248 Obv. Designer: William J. Krawczewicz **Rev. Designer:** Dean McMullen **Obverse:** World Cup trophy **Reverse:** World Cup 94 logo

Date	UNC Mintage	Proof Mintage	MS-65	Prf-65
1994W	22,464	—	375	—
1994W	—	89,619	—	385

1996 Olympics - Stadium.
KM# 265 Obverse: Atlanta Stadium and logo **Reverse:** Eagle advancing right

Date	UNC Mintage	Proof Mintage	MS-65	Prf-65
1995W	10,579	—	2,400	—
1995W	—	43,124	—	575

1996 Olympics - Torch runner.
KM# 261 Obverse: Torch runner, Atlanta skyline and logo in background **Reverse:** Eagle advancing right

Date	UNC Mintage	Proof Mintage	MS-65	Prf-65
1995W	14,675	—	900	—
1995W	—	57,442	—	375

Civil War.
KM# 256 Obv. Designer: Don Troiani **Rev. Designer:** Alfred Maletsky **Obverse:** Bugler on horseback right **Reverse:** Ealge on shield

Date	UNC Mintage	Proof Mintage	MS-65	Prf-65
1995W	12,735	—	925	—
1995W	—	55,246	—	395

1996 Olympics - Cauldron.
KM# 270 Obverse: Torch bearer lighting cauldron
Reverse: Atlanta Olympics logo flanked by laurel

Date	UNC Mintage	Proof Mintage	MS-65	Prf-65
1996W	9,210	—	2,650	—
1996W	—	38,555	—	575

Jackie Robinson.
KM# 280 Obv. Designer: William C. Cousins
Rev. Designer: James M. Peed **Obverse:** Robinson
head right **Reverse:** Legend on baseball

Date	UNC Mintage	Proof Mintage	MS-65	Prf-65
1997W	5,202	—	3,900	—
1997W	24,072	—	—	575

1996 Olympics - Flag bearer.
KM# 274 Obverse: Flag bearer advancing
Reverse: Atlanta Olympic logo flanked by laurel

Date	UNC Mintage	Proof Mintage	MS-65	Prf-65
1996W	9,174	—	2,650	—
1996W	—	32,886	—	635

George Washington Death Bicentennial.
KM# 300 Designer: Laura G. Fraser.
Obverse: Washington's head right **Reverse:** Eagle
with wings outstreatched

Date	UNC Mintage	Proof Mintage	MS-65	Prf-65
1999W	22,511	—	395	—
1999W	—	41,693	—	375

Smithsonian Institution 150th Anniversary.
KM# 277 Obv. Designer: Alfred Maletsky
Rev. Designer: T. James Ferrell **Obverse:** Smithson
bust left **Reverse:** Sunburst museum logo

Date	UNC Mintage	Proof Mintage	MS-65	Prf-65
1996W	9,068	—	900	—
1996W	21,840	—	—	495

Capitol Visitor Center.
KM# 326 Designer: Elizabeth Jones. **Obverse:**
Column at right **Reverse:** First Capital building

Date	UNC Mintage	Proof Mintage	MS-65	Prf-65
2001W	6,761	—	1,750	—
2001W	—	27,652	—	420

Franklin Delano Roosevelt.
KM# 282 Obv. Designer: T. James Ferrell
Rev. Designer: James M. Peed and Thomas D.
Rogers, Sr. **Obverse:** Roosevlet bust right
Reverse: Eagle shield

Date	UNC Mintage	Proof Mintage	MS-65	Prf-65
1997W	11,894	—	1,600	—
1997W	29,233	—	—	395

2002 Winter Olympics.
KM# 337 Designer: Donna Weaver. **Obverse:** Salt
Lake City Olympics logo **Reverse:** Stylized cauldron

Date	UNC Mintage	Proof Mintage	MS-65	Prf-65
2002W	10,585	—	440	—
2002W	—	32,877	—	365

San Francisco Mint Museum.
KM# 395 Obverse: Front entrance façade
Reverse: Eagle as on 1860's $5. Gold

Date	UNC Mintage	Proof Mintage	MS-65	Prf-65
2006S	16,230	—	285	—
2006S	—	41,517	—	295

Jamestown - 400th Anniversary.
KM# 406 Obverse: Settler and Native American
Reverse: Jamestown Memorial Church ruins

Date	UNC Mintage	Proof Mintage	MS-65	Prf-65
2007W	18,843	—	345	—
2007W	—	47,050	—	345

American Bald Eagle.
KM# 440 Obverse: Two eagles on branch
Reverse: Eagle with shield

Date	UNC Mintage	Proof Mintage	MS-65	Prf-65
2008W	13,467	—	285	—
2008W	—	59,269	—	300

$10 (EAGLE)

1984 Olympics.
KM# 211 Obv. Designer: James M. Peed and John
Mercanti **Rev. Designer:** John Mercanti **Obverse:**
Male and female runner with torch **Reverse:**
Heraldic eagle **Diameter:** 27 **Weight:** 16.7180 g.
Composition: 0.9000 Gold, 0.4837 oz. AGW.

Date	UNC Mintage	Proof Mintage	MS-65	Prf-65
1984W	75,886	—	610	—
1984P	—	33,309	—	650
1984D	—	34,533	—	650
1984S	—	48,551	—	650
1984W	—	381,085	—	650

Library of Congress.
KM# 312 Obv. Designer: John Mercanti
Rev. Designer: Thomas D. Rogers, Sr. **Obverse:**
Torch and partial facade **Reverse:** Stylized eagle
within laurel wreath **Weight:** 16.2590 g.
Composition: Bi-Metallic

Date	UNC Mintage	Proof Mintage	MS-65	Prf-65
2000W	6,683	—	5,950	—
2000W	—	27,167	—	1,075

First Flight Centennial.
KM# 350 Designer: Donna Weaver.
Obverse: Orvile and Wilbur Wright busts facing
Reverse: Wright flyer and eagle **Weight:** 16.7180 g.
Composition: 0.9000 Gold, 0.4837 oz. AGW.

Date	UNC Mintage	Proof Mintage	MS-65	Prf-65
2003P	10,129	—	650	—
2003P	—	21,846	—	650

$20 (DOUBLE EAGLE)

KM# 464 Designer: Augustus Saint-Gaudens.
Obverse: Liberty holding torch, walking forward
Reverse: Eagle in flight left, sunrise in background
Diameter: 27 **Composition:** 0.9990 Gold AGW.
Notes: Ultra high relief

Date	UNC Mintage	Proof Mintage	MS-65	Prf-65
2009	115,178	—	—	1,275